Longing For Revival

From Holy Discontent To Breakthrough Faith

James Choung
Ryan Pfeiffer

16pt

Copyright Page from the Original Book

InterVarsity Press
P.O. Box 1400, Downers Grove, IL 60515-1426
ivpress.com
email@ivpress.com

©2020 by James Choung and Ryan Pfeiffer

All rights reserved. No part of this book may be reproduced in any form without written permission from InterVarsity Press.

InterVarsity Press® is the book-publishing division of InterVarsity Christian Fellowship/USA®, a movement of students and faculty active on campus at hundreds of universities, colleges, and schools of nursing in the United States of America, and a member movement of the International Fellowship of Evangelical Students. For information about local and regional activities, visit intervarsity.org.

All Scripture quotations, unless otherwise indicated, are taken from The Holy Bible, New International Version®, NIV®. Copyright © 1973, 1978, 1984, 2011 by Biblica, Inc.™ Used by permission of Zondervan. All rights reserved worldwide. www.zondervan.com. The "NIV" and "New International Version" are trademarks registered in the United States Patent and Trademark Office by Biblica, Inc.™

While any stories in this book are true, some names and identifying information may have been changed to protect the privacy of individuals.

Cover design and image composite: David Fassett
Interior design: Daniel van Loon
Images: canvas close up: © rawpixel.com / pexels.com
    blurred background: © Pixabay / pexels.com
    explosive fire: © Skitterphoto / pexels.com
    sparkler: © Suvan Chowdhury / pexels.com
    colored concrete: © FWStudio / pexels.com
    wave curl: © Steve Wyper / Getty Images

TABLE OF CONTENTS

Intro: WHY REVIVAL?	ii
PART ONE: DEFINING REVIVAL	
Chapter One: REVIVAL FOR THE REST OF US	3
Chapter Two: FROM HOLY DISCONTENT TO CRUCIFIED HOPE	38
Chapter Three: FROM CRISIS OF FAITH TO BREAKTHROUGH FAITH	64
PART TWO: EXPERIENCING REVIVAL	
Chapter Four: CONSECRATION	95
Chapter Five: CALLING	129
Chapter Six: CONTENDING	162
Chapter Seven: CHARACTER	195
PART THREE: LEADING REVIVAL	
Chapter Eight: ALL PLAY	221
Chapter Nine: MYSTERY AND STRATEGY PARADOX	247
Chapter Ten: COMMUNAL DISCERNMENT	279
Chapter Eleven: KINGDOM BUILDING	305
Outro: ALREADY AND NOT YET	327
ACKNOWLEDGMENTS	344
NOTES	353
PRAISE FOR LONGING FOR REVIVAL	389
ABOUT THE AUTHORS	396

DEDICATION

JAMES:
To Jamie—
Shine among them like stars in the sky as you hold firmly to the word of life.

RYAN:
To my children:
Diego, Ramón, and Cellia, and the next generation of Christians—
May God release a mighty movement of his Spirit through you!

Intro

WHY REVIVAL?

Renewal is this process that God keeps taking us on that he's written into the fabric of the cosmos, because humans must always choose to choose God again.
MARK SAYERS, "SECULAR SALVATION SCHEMA"

Come, ... and you will see.
JESUS OF NAZARETH, JOHN 1:39

Let me (James) start this book with a confession.

I grew up spiritually in a Korean American immigrant church, located in a suburban enclave just north of Seattle. The Christian faith ran deep in my Korean family lines, and my parents brought their love of Jesus with them when they immigrated to America in the '60s. They actually lived so faithfully that I could collect little evidence to build a case of hypocrisy against them.

And they prayerfully sought to pass their legacy of faith on to me.

So at least twice a week, my little brother and I would find ourselves at church. My parents were involved in everything from church leadership to meal preparations to youth ministry to the choir.

In this setting, the word *revival* was used often. It would be slapped on any event outside a Sunday worship service. Guest speaker? Revival meeting. A weekend retreat? The whole weekend would be called a revival meeting. We sought revival, sang songs about revival, proclaimed that revival would come in this generation (how many "prophets" should we stone for the last one?), and it had a way of stirring up the passions and imagination of everyone who was as young as me.

So much expectation and promise seemed to be loaded into that word, as if the mere mention of it would bring a fresh wave of the Holy Spirit.

Frankly, it felt manipulative.

In reaction, my soul was set against that word, so much so that when I accepted my first-ever invitation to be a conference speaker outside of my own ministry context, I had the gall to preach against revival.

I remember being high up in the mountains above Colorado Springs. At 9,124 feet, I had to drink lots of water to stave off the headaches and nausea of altitude sickness. The air was so thin that a flight of stairs easily doubled me over. When I went up to speak, I was surrounded by a forest of Douglas fir and spruce, and they had ironically set up a huge canopy tent in a grassy clearing, like the American revival meetings of old.

On that night a couple of decades ago, I came with a mission: I'd dress down revival until it was shown to be an empty, naked promise.

Here's a snippet from that talk:

> Ask the Lord what it means to be a part of this forcefully, advancing kingdom. When he tells you what to do, be faithful. This way, you wouldn't ask for revivals anymore. I must say that I get really bummed out when people pray for revival...

We don't have to pray for revival, but we need to be faithful.

The problem is, I think that talk might still be persuasive today.

But now I think I had it all wrong. If you heard me teach that evening, I ask for your forgiveness. I now believe we should long for revival.

Can't We Just Be Faithful?

Why can't we just be faithful? The author of Hebrews wrote about faithful witnesses: "All these people were still living by faith when they died. They did not receive the things promised; they only saw them and welcomed them from a distance, admitting that they were foreigners and strangers on earth." They needed a breakthrough, but they didn't see it in their lifetimes.

It's true that some promises won't be fulfilled on this side of history. Embracing our alien status is healthy at times. It's the tension we live in. It's mysterious. So it makes sense to be enmcouraged to be faithful, like "these people" who "were still living by faith when they died."

So we need to be faithful. Deeply faithful.

But I fear that in our modern day, being faithful can mean something else. I wonder if it means something closer to "hang in there, because things will never change." It can feel fatalistic. Dictionaries support this idea: faithful is defined as "steadfast in affection or allegiance." Faithfulness, as one book title tells us, is "a long obedience in the same direction." We're to remain steady and keep on keepin' on, right?

But in our attempts to be faithful, have we lost a sense of hope?

In *The Shawshank Redemption*, arguably one of the best movies of the 1990s, Andy is sentenced to two life sentences for a crime he didn't commit. He is regularly assaulted by other inmates and lives precariously under the unjust thumb of the warden. As an act of rebellion, he plays Mozart's *The Marriage of Figaro* over the public address system, and as a result, he's punished with two weeks in solitary confinement.

Afterward, he tells his inmate friends over lunch that it was worth it, "the easiest time I ever did." He explains that the music was in him, reminding him that what he saw wasn't all that was—that the music provided hope. And it's with that remark that Red, a fellow inmate, bristles.

"Let me tell you something, my friend," Red says. "Hope is a dangerous thing. Hope can drive a man insane. It's got no use on the inside. You'd better get used to that idea."

Have we gotten used to that idea?

Perhaps you are single, and you really want to be married. Does being faithful mean that you automatically give up this dream? Or perhaps you love and trust Jesus but your family doesn't, and you really want them to know the God you love. But they're clearly hostile to your faith or any spiritual conversations. It's been years, even decades. Wouldn't it be wise just to guard your heart?

Maybe you wish your faith community felt more spiritually alive. Couldn't they at least try to live out the teachings of Jesus? Perhaps you're part of a church where your pastor had a moral failure and left the ministry, and you're left to pick up the pieces. Should you just remain faithful while silently succumbing to the thought that nothing will ever change?

What if a racial incident flares up tensions between ethnic communities on your campus or in your community? What if you're frustrated with the state of our country and its leadership, or just frustrated with your relatives' justifications of their political views? You might be sick at the thought of the rich getting richer while the poor get poorer. What if you long for the day when our families, communities, cities, nations, and the world would fall in love with Jesus, and let him finally be the leader of everything he deserves to be? Isn't that unhelpful, even irresponsible, fantasizing?

Maturity seems to say to lower your hopes. Don't dream for something better, just in case it doesn't happen. Why open yourself to having your heart trampled over and over again?

The Bible tells a story of a wealthy yet barren Shunammite woman who thought the same way. She was generous, showing the prophet Elisha great hospitality whenever he was in town. At any time, he could count on her to offer a meal and a furnished room for the night. To repay her kindness, he tells her that she'll have a son within a year.

She replies, "Please, man of God, don't mislead your servant!"

In other words, don't mess with me! You're cruel if you're playing with my emotions.

But it actually comes to pass. She gives birth to a son, and the child grows. But one day, he complains about pain in his head and eventually dies on her lap. She immediately reaches out for Elisha, and her voice seems to be trembling with a mix of anger and despair: "Did I ask you for a son, my lord? ... Didn't I tell you, 'Don't raise my hopes'?"

She almost seems to be saying, it's better if you hadn't promised anything at all. Don't get my hopes up, and then dash them on the rocks. It's too much to bear. Biblical wisdom literature seems to agree: "Hope deferred makes the heart sick."

So we'd rather assassinate hope. It's too dangerous.

And just be "faithful."

But the author of Hebrews writes about faith in this way: "Faith is confidence in what we hope for and assurance about what we do not see. This is what the ancients were commended for."

There seems to be a deep connection between faith and hope. If we're being faithful in a biblical way, we're also hopeful because hope is faith applied to the future.

I wonder if we've settled for faith without hope. We've eased into a sort of fatalism. On the other hand we know it's foolish to have hope without faith, which is mere optimism.

But what if we had faith that isn't afraid to hope again?

A Change of Mind

Sometimes we trade hope for something else. Hope can feel too passive. It trusts and waits that something or someone else can fix our problems and find a way.

So we often try, instead, to take things into our own hands. It's tempting to rely on a technical or strategic fix for almost everything. And sure, sometimes, that might be precisely what we need.

But we know deep down that spiritual breakthrough won't come from the latest marketing scheme, the most effective social media strategy, the strongest preaching series, or even the best tactics of vibrant ministry.

We need something far deeper. We need revival.

Now, if hope is a dangerous word, then revival can feel outright murderous.

Revival elicits strong reactions. It's hard to ignore. Maybe for you, it's the longing that has filled countless nights of prayer. It grabs you in the gut, in the deepest parts of your soul. You have the kind of faith that wants revival to sweep through your life, your community, your nation, and the world. And you won't rest until you get it.

Or perhaps, the talk of revival, like Newtonian physics, creates an equal and opposite reaction, increasing the anxiety and fear that we'll "shake and bake" in church aisles and say God "showed up." A historian wrote, "Aren't revivals quirky folk rituals associated with rural America and nineteenth-century camp meetings? Didn't they pass out of fashion with hula hoops and Edsels?" You might be worried that youthful or grandiose passions will be stoked, only to eventually fizzle out. Perhaps most insidiously, like the Shunammite woman, you're afraid that hope will be ratcheted up, only to disappoint in the end.

Ryan and I have felt all of those things. I preached against this word, remember?

So when Ryan started bringing up revival with me a few years ago, I have to admit my heart was as open as a fist. I had heard it all before. But we had been in ministry together for almost two decades, serving college students throughout the country. We had witnessed a local revival together as over 4,300 students in San Diego County would give their lives over to Jesus over the span of a decade and a half, and many would mature to become world changers in his name. I just didn't want to call it revival.

We were already good friends and trusted ministry partners, and we had seen God move powerfully. So little by little, I started to listen more to what he was saying. As we went along, we invited others to learn about and pray toward revival. We were deeply surprised to find that our movement was listening as well. I serve as a national leader for InterVarsity Christian Fellowship USA, leading strategy and innovation, and through much prayer and discussion, our national movement is now chasing this calling for the next decade: "Longing for revival, we catalyze movements that call every corner of every campus to follow Jesus."

We know that we're not going to strategize our way to revival. Instead, we need to learn how to long for revival and help steward it, if it comes.

Much of this book comes from Ryan's research, thinking, and prayers, and I've come along to nuance the ideas and help broadcast these teachings far and wide. We've both taught this material often, and as we've met almost every week in the writing of this book—spending much of our time in prayer as well as discussing the book—we've found ourselves strongly encouraged. So we hope that this writing represents not two voices but the Spirit's one voice through us and that it will be an encouragement to you.

This book, then, is an invitation: Will you long for revival with us?

Why Revival?

It's important to long for revival for a few reasons: First, it has some biblical basis. The psalmist prays, "Will you not revive us again, that your people may rejoice in you?" It's right there: a prayer for the revival of the Jewish people and their faith in God. We'll make a stronger biblical case throughout the book for the concept of revival, but for now, wouldn't that be a great prayer for the Christian church?

It is also historic. From Pentecost to the present day, revivals have dotted the timeline of Christian history. There were times when Christian spirituality seemed to recede into the background, but when revivals arrived, new movements sprouted up that brought spiritual vitality back to the church—from the Franciscans to the Moravians to the Pentecostals to the Korean Presbyterians to the East Africans.

It could be strategic. Eighteenth-century pastor Jonathan Edwards saw the strategic nature of revival. As recounted by professor Richard Lovelace, Edwards believed, "Every major advance of the kingdom of God on earth is signaled and brought about by a general outpouring of the Holy Spirit."

And in the twenty-first century, Christianity hasn't died away, although much of its center has shifted away from the Western world to Africa, Asia, and South America. In his book *Global Awakening,* Mark Shaw shows that Christianity is surging worldwide, and he believes that revival is the main delivery system for this tremendous growth: "Global revivals ... are at the heart of the global resurgence of Christianity."

Revivals are happening all around the world. And I don't want to be someone who's on the outside looking in. What if we were understanding and preparing ourselves, so that if revival were to come through our lives or land, we could be ready to be a part of it?

Perhaps more importantly, *revival* is a powerful word.

Our culture tries to co-opt the word. The word *revive* is used in all kinds of marketing from skin care to skateboards, craft beers to conferences, massage spas to mattresses. Even pop albums are titled *Revival.* It's almost a commercial cliché.

But more deeply, to revive something means that it must've been either dead or close to dead. Life had seeped away. Lungs stopped breathing. Hearts beat no longer. Flesh rotted away so that all that could be seen was a valley of dry bones. Something died within us or around us.

When something is revived, however, it comes back to life.

It's resuscitated.

In faith-speak, it's resurrected.

We seek that kind of resurrection in our lives, communities, societies, and ultimately, throughout the world, because right now, much of it reeks of death.

The world needs leaders who are resuscitated, resurrected, revived. No revival has happened in history without revived people. We need leaders who know how to help others be revived, and that's not going to happen merely with good management principles, solid plans and execution, or clever social media campaigns. Sure, they can be important and helpful, but they are merely the skin and bones. Revival needs to be infused with breath, blood, soul, and life.

And that only comes through God's Spirit.

But before we scare anyone off, we also know that revival without good, wise, feet-on-the-ground strategic leadership will quickly fizzle. It's the difference between a weekend retreat and an ongoing work of God's Spirit among us.

We seek the intersection of strategic and spiritual leadership that leads to revival, where structures and mystery meet.

We need form and fire.

We need revival for the rest of us.

And sure, we can't manufacture revivals. We definitely can't make them happen. But they can break out. And for revivals to last, they must be led.

That's where this book is going: If revival leadership is the kind of ministry leadership needed before and during revival, what would it look like to exercise revival leadership in this day and age? This book is not a history book on past revivals, nor is it an analysis of broad-scale dynamics for revival. Those volumes have been written. Instead, we want to equip you to prepare for and lead revival effectively.

So the framework for revival leadership consists of these three parts:

Part 1: Defining Revival addresses your head. What is revival? What are the biblical foundations for the idea of revival? What is the process of revival in you and through you? In this section, we'll present a definition of revival for our day and identify a core revival process called the breakthrough U curve.

Part 2: Experiencing Revival addresses your heart. Once you grasp a rudimentary idea of revival, then how do you start seeking it? How do you prepare for it, if it comes? What would it look like to experience revival personally? In this part, we'll guide you through revival practices—consecration, calling, contending, and growing in character—to long for revival personally. Because revivals are first experienced, and then given away.

Part 3: Leading Revival addresses your hands. Once you've experienced revival, how do you lead it for others? What values and skills will be necessary to help a moment become a movement? In these chapters, we'll highlight four key revival leadership concepts: everyone gets to play, lean into both mystery and strategy, learn to hear from God together, and seek the kingdom instead of an empire. The work of revival is God's, but we'll try to make the case that for revivals to thrive, they must also be led.

Our hope is that if revival comes, this book will have equipped you so that instead of missing out, you will find yourself experiencing and leading in it. We hope that by the time you finish reading, you too will also long for revival.

Discussion Questions

1. What comes to mind when you hear the word *revival?* How does it make you feel?
2. In what ways has hope been elusive in your expression of faith?
3. In what ways would you like to see revival in your own life?
4. How would you like to see revival play out in the communities you belong to?

PART ONE
DEFINING REVIVAL

Chapter One

REVIVAL FOR THE REST OF US

A revival, then, really means days of heaven upon earth.
MARTYN LLOYD-JONES, *REVIVAL*

Will you not revive us again, that your people may rejoice in you?
SONS OF KORAH, PSALM 85:6

While he was in college, a friend of ours, Sam, once passed up an offer to go out for dinner. The father of one of his roommates was in town and offered to take the entire apartment out for dinner, but Sam was tired from a long day. While he declined, his other roommate, Jerome, didn't miss a beat taking up the offer.

When Jerome returned, he said to Sam, "You won't believe where we went to eat!"

"Where'd you go?"

"To the most extravagant restaurant I've ever been to."

Then he began to describe his meal: S.Pellegrino, not water. Two different appetizers. Then, lobster. Steak. Duck. The best wine. Chocolate dessert. And, they had their own dedicated waiter throughout the meal. Total cost? $450 for four, even when the restaurant had thrown in the appetizers.

And, of course, his roommate's dad had covered the bill.

Sam had one definition of dinner in his mind, but dinner turned out to be something far better than he had imagined.

What if it's like that with the word *revival?* What if we're turning down "dinner" before finding out what revival truly is?

So before judgments are cast, let's define revival.

Defining Revival

Not only does revival have a wide range of definitions, it is also one of several terms describing similar spiritual dynamics—such as renewal and awakening. Although some may make distinctions between these three terms, we don't. Richard Lovelace, a scholar on evangelical revival, offered the same conclusion: "Renewal, revival and awakening trace back to biblical metaphors for the infusion of spiritual life in Christian experience by the Holy Spirit. Usually they are used synonymously."

So what is revival?

The first set of definitions we found is clustered around personal or corporate reinvigoration of our spiritual experience. Charles Finney, a minister and leader in the Second Great Awakening, defined revival as "a renewed conviction of sin and repentance, followed by an intense desire to live in obedience to God." Mid-twentieth-century British pastor Martyn Lloyd-Jones described it as "a period of unusual blessing and activity in the life of the Christian Church."

What they all are saying in so many words is this: in revivals, faith becomes "white-hot." And although we liked these definitions as far as they went, we yearned to include more specifics about how revival would be expressed and how it might spill over to those who don't identify as Christian.

Others add more specifics to their definitions. In his book, *Revivals: Their Laws and Leaders,* James Burns highlights the amount of people involved: "Large numbers of persons who have been dead or indifferent to spiritual realities then become intensely awakened to them." Pastor Tim Keller offered one along the same lines: "A season in which a whole body of believers experience gospel renewal together." Lovelace adds a missional element: "Broad-scale movements of the Holy Spirit's work in renewing spiritual vitality in the church and in fostering its expansion in mission and evangelism." Author Mark Shaw adds a societal effect to his definition: "Global revivals are charismatic people movements that transform their world by translating Christian truth and transferring power."

We liked these additions as well but wanted to see them come together in a single definition. But I'd like to pause here and ask, Whatever misgivings you might have about the word *revival,* if you saw these characteristics or marks of revival in your faith communities, wouldn't you welcome them?

But yes, the range of definitions can make your eyes swim.

That led us down a path to find a more accessible definition of revival. Could we capture a similar range of definitions in a simpler way, while also coming up with something that could be welcomed by more faith communities?

Could we define revival for the rest of us?

So we researched what revival looked like in history, learned from its dynamics, prayed about it, and attempted to tackle a definition that might be helpful to our movement. After nine months, we landed on a definition for revival:

> A season of breakthroughs
> in word, deed, and power
> that ushers in a new normal
> of kingdom experience and
> fruitfulness

Let's unpack it.

A Season of Breakthroughs

The first line, "a season of breakthroughs," avoids defining revival by a singular event. We say breakthrough*s*, not breakthrough. If revival could include any one-off experience, then it's not very useful as a term. For example, let's say I just had a powerful experience with God last night. Should that be considered revival? We didn't want a definition that could too easily speak of any single spiritual experience.

The implications are enormous. For example, the day of Pentecost—on its own—would not be considered a revival. Wait, what? Yes, the Holy Spirit surely swept through the community of believers, and three thousand people and their families were baptized into the Christian faith. Still, we wouldn't consider that revival.

Not yet.

But in Acts 2:42-47, Pentecost marks the beginning of a fledgling faith community that starts to have its own set of rhythms setting it apart. It has moved beyond a moment to a movement. It's beginning to become a revival at that point.

Then, add an Acts 3 healing, an Acts 4 filling of the Holy Spirit, an Acts 5 supernatural intervention of discipline, and an Acts 6 move of justice to empower ethnic minorities—and the revival is growing. The whole book of Acts describes revival.

It wasn't just one breakthrough but a season of breakthroughs. And it doesn't last forever. That's also important. It's a "season."

Consider it as nature's rhythm. Springtime comes after winter, fall after summer. There's a blossoming, then a retreat. In the same way, throughout history, revivals ended. They came for a limited time—sometimes for three months and other times for three decades—but when they came, God broke through long enough to create a new normal.

Also, the boundaries between seasons aren't always rigid; they can be fuzzy. In the throes of winter, spring already has its seeds in place. Potential lies dormant under the snow, ready to break through. When spring starts to arrive, a few sunny days surprise us. A warm gentle breeze carries the first scents of new life. But it can retreat, and winter delays spring's full bloom.

It's that kind of peekaboo experience that can capture these seasons of spiritual awakening. At first, the signs can be shy and fickle, but they eventually grow stronger and more consistent like the rising temperatures and longer days. Soon enough, we find ourselves in the embrace of a new season that sweeps us up into its characteristic joys and wonders.

But even with their ebbs and flows, revivals, when added up, "are at the heart of the global resurgence of Christianity."

With just one line of our definition, we change the quality of revival that we seek.

We don't just seek a single breakthrough but a season of breakthroughs.

In Word, Deed, and Power

If the first line of our definition expands the length of revival, the second line expands its breadth. These breakthroughs happen "in word, deed, and power." The idea comes from Paul himself in his letter to the Romans. In chapter 15, he offers a summary of his ministry:

> Therefore I glory in Christ Jesus in my service to God. I will not venture to speak of anything except what Christ has accomplished through me in leading the Gentiles to obey God by what I have *said* and *done*—by the *power* of signs and wonders, through the *power* of the Spirit of God. So from Jerusalem all the way around to Illyricum, I have *fully proclaimed* the gospel of Christ.

How can Paul claim that he "fully proclaimed" the gospel of Christ? What did he mean? A few interpretations exist, and the most likely way to read this is that he fulfilled his mandate to plant strategic churches in the region described "from Jerusalem all the way around to Illyricum."

But "fully proclaimed" could also point to the nature of his proclamation. A Greek lexicon offers this definition:

"to relate fully the content of a message." And in this passage, one way that he fully proclaimed the gospel was through word, deed, and power.

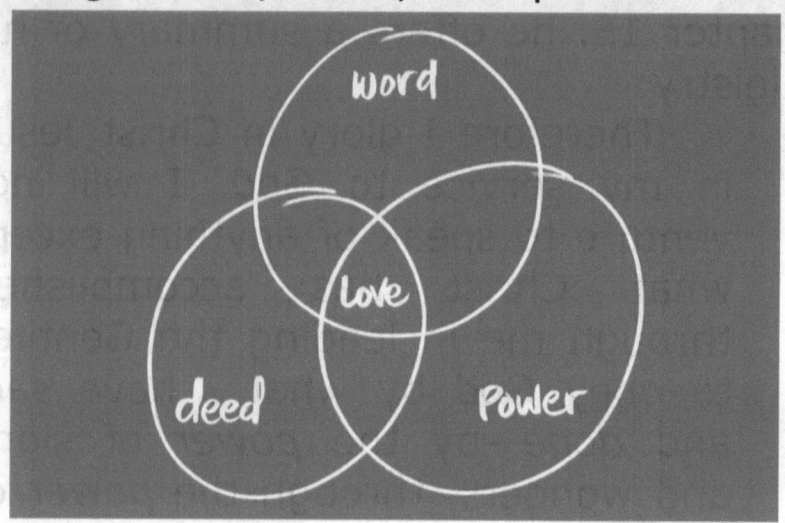

Figure 1. The full proclamation of the gospel

By word, we mean the expression of the gospel through biblical teaching and preaching. By deed, we mean the expression of the gospel in compassion and justice. By power, we mean the expression of the gospel in miraculous or explicitly supernatural ways.

But how many faith communities can claim to fully express word, deed, and power? Most offer one. Fewer offer two. But all three?

Yet mature Christian revivals often had all three.

It's easy to see how having only one of these three expressions of the gospel can stunt revival in our hearts and communities. Word without deed or power could potentially lead to a privatized kind of faith or a dead legalism. A breakthrough in deed without word or power could become a social justice cause without explaining the source of hope or knowing the sense of its power. A breakthrough in power without word or deed can press into an excessive show of emotionalism or an unhealthy hunger for a heavenly experience that does no earthly good.

When these three come together in love, however, they have a way of keeping a healthy balance between the expressions of the Christian gospel.

But what often happens is that the word-centered folks denigrate deed-centered folks, thinking that they do good works but don't have theological grounding, and also look down on the power-centered folks as people who chase experiences without being rooted in the Word. And deed-centered folks may judge word-centered folks as pandering to dead orthodoxy while wondering when the power-centered folks will stop chasing an otherworldly, spiritual high and start seeking justice. Power-centered folks wonder if the word-centered folks are guilty of "having a form of godliness but denying its power," while believing that the deed-centered folks are burnt out and angry because they don't tap into the life of the Spirit.

What was meant to work together, we often pull apart.

By holding these three jointly, there is room for all in revival. And in fact, we believe all are needed for revival to reach its full capacity.

Of course, all of these circles don't have to play out at the first flush of revival. Historically, revival can come through any one of these circles.

The First Great Awakening came primarily through the word circle, where John Wesley preached to miners and taught the Methodists to seek greater holiness through the support of Christian community. At the turn of the thirteenth century, the Franciscans started out primarily through the deed circle, as their founder, Francis of Assisi, cared for lepers and embraced voluntary poverty. The Pentecostal movement at the turn of the twentieth century came primarily through the power circle, as the Holy Spirit fell on a multiracial community at Azusa Street.

But as revivals mature, they start taking on the other values. The Methodists started as Bible teachers and preachers, but they would be open to power as manifestations of the Holy Spirit would disrupt Wesley's meetings, and they moved into deed with their concern for the poor and lower classes. Although known for their vows of poverty, the Franciscans leaned into the word circle through communal Bible studies and preaching the gospel throughout the world, and the power circle would be expressed through mystical experiences of such ecstasy that they "lay on the ground like dead men." The Pentecostal movement, as it grew, preached to a packed house daily on Azusa Street, pressing further into word, and quickly moved into the deed circle as people from different ethnic, gender, and class groups were empowered together.

Revivals, as they mature, move toward the center.

They exhibit word, deed, and power in love.

In 1929, Ugandan healthcare worker Simeoni Nsibambi met with a burned-out British doctor and missionary, Joe Church, to seek God for a fresh infusion of the Spirit. After two days of intense Bible study and prayer, they experienced what they referred to as "a share in the power of Pentecost." For the next four decades, the East African revival poured all the way down to South Africa, and then over to other continents. The word and power revival expressed deed when African Christian leaders and European missionaries publicly confessed racial pride and invited others to do the same at their gatherings. One African attendee said, "I have never before seen any white man admit he had any sins." Those touched by this revival actively promoted justice, fought corruption, and elevated Christian ethics over tribal loyalty, some paying for these outspoken views with their lives.

The power circle and the Holy Spirit. InterVarsity Christian Fellowship USA, as an evangelical organization, has a large word circle (see figure 1). We use manuscript Bible study from our smallest to largest gatherings, where we pull out colored pencils to mark up our copy of the Scripture passage, making careful observations, asking rigorous questions, and interpreting the text to find genuine applications. It's one of the best things we do.

Our deed circle is more medium-sized. Our students spend their spring breaks to serve in projects like ServeUp in the aftermath of Hurricanes Katrina and Harvey, and we include students and faculty of every ethnicity and culture. Our history is rich with stories of our staff championing racially integrated Bible studies and camps in the '40s, a decade before the civil rights movement began. And our alumni have done amazing things for the common good, such as leading an organization that serves prisoners and their families and starting a movement that fights slavery and injustice all around the world.

But, in full confession, our power circle is small. We have pockets of staff and students who are open to the Holy Spirit moving in power, and we're growing in it. But, it's still not that widespread.

If mature revivals reflect all three circles in harmony and balance, then our movement needs to be more open to the power of God's Spirit. We wonder if that's generally true for many Western believers. And as we look back in history, the revival landscape was often flooded with an openness to the Holy Spirit—whether in intimacy or miraculous power.

And we're aware that there have been spiritual excesses and abuses in the name of the Holy Spirit. You may have personally witnessed or experienced some of them, causing you great harm and pain. We don't minimize the trauma that many have experienced. As we move forward, we must continually check and balance our power experiences with word and deed.

Still, the Scriptures say, "Do not quench the Spirit."

To prepare ourselves for revival, we'll need leaders who see the desire for greater intimacy with the Spirit as a sign of awakening bubbling up in a generation desiring more of God and who resist the temptation to respond with a knee-jerk reaction against the Sprit, fueled by fear of all that could go wrong. They could offer wise, biblical, experienced, grounded, and courageous mentoring so that a new move of God can be birthed.

Could we be more like the Bereans in Acts 17:11, who "received the message with great eagerness and examined the Scriptures every day to see if what Paul said was true"? As you read on, you might read something that pushes your comfort zone a bit. And while you test what we write through the lens of Scripture, would you consider having an open heart and mind to what the Spirit might say?

Love is at the center. And one more caveat: all of this—word, deed, and power—needs to operate in love. It's almost too obvious to be stated, and for that reason we didn't include it in the definition. But still, we didn't want you to miss it. The Scriptures warn us that anything done without love is worthless. First Corinthians 13 explains this well through word, deed, and power:

> If I speak in the tongues of men or of angels [power], but do not have love, I am only a resounding gong or a clanging cymbal. If I have the gift of prophecy and can fathom all mysteries and all knowledge [word and power], and if I have a faith that can move mountains, but do not have love, I am nothing. If I give all I possess to the poor and give over my body to hardship that I may boast [deed], but do not have love, I gain nothing.

It's actually easy to exercise word, deed, and power without love. We can preach the text rightly but have little care for our audience. We could lead protests against injustices but hate our oppressors. We might pray for miracles but do it for our own glory. And if we do, word, deed, and power become dangerous and abusive.

Our gifts are most powerful and effective, however, when expressed through love, because that is who God is.

That Ushers In a New Normal

The third line of our definition highlights the result of revivals: "That ushers in a new normal." These breakthroughs aren't merely about the experience, but they should create a new expectancy of what God can do in us, through us, and around us.

Imagine being part of a faith community where it's rare to have someone decide to follow Jesus for the first time. It's like spotting an endangered species: "See the new Christian grazing in the savannah..." But then, something changes, and families start to get baptized to mark the start of their newfound faith every three months or so. That changes expectations. It becomes a new normal to have families come to faith every once in a while. And because that happens, it doesn't seem impossible to think of someone coming to faith every month. In fact, it would be disappointing if the community went back to seeing no one come to faith anymore.

It's a new normal.

This may be the most important piece of the definition: revivals should create a new normal. They weren't given so that we can just go back to the way things were. They were given so that our faith can have capacity for more, to hope for more, to seek more of God's kingdom.

Back in 2001, I (Ryan) stood in front of over a hundred students for our weekly InterVarsity worship gathering at the University of California, San Diego. At the end of a message about Jesus' love for lost people, I asked a simple question: "How many of you have ever seen a friend come to faith and have been a part of that process?"

The room went dead silent.

After an awkward ten seconds, three students sheepishly raised their hands.

Only three. The dots connected before my eyes: virtually no one had ever seen it happen. We might as well have been asking students to pray for the dead to rise. It was no surprise—at that point in the fall semester, no one had come to faith through our community.

So, I pulled together a small team of campus ministers, and the three of us would encourage and equip students to lead their friends to Jesus. We prayed, we taught, and we modeled. By the end of that academic year, by God's grace, 28 students started to follow Jesus!

Emboldened, the following year we began praying for 100 students to come to faith. It was crazy: only one campus in our sixty-year history as a national movement had ever seen more than 100 students come to faith in a year, and that one had Billy Graham preaching on campus. Yet with a new normal, we grew in confidence that God could use students to make a significant impact on our campus—even without Billy Graham!

Two years later, we saw 104 students come to faith through UCSD

InterVarsity in a single year. The following year: 107 students. When I asked again how many people had been part of helping a friend come to faith, over half the students in the room raised a hand. A palpable faith had energized the community with newfound purpose and joy.

After one of our weekly gatherings where fifteen students had stood to dedicate their lives to following Jesus, a freshman excitedly told me, "It feels like every week we are having a revival. I used to only feel that when I went to a Christian camp, but it would fade as soon as I got home. Here, it's like it never fades. It just keeps going from week to week!"

Of Kingdom Experience and Fruitfulness

We round out our definition with the fourth line, which describes the dimensions of revival: "of kingdom experience and fruitfulness."

It's in and out. It's internal and external.

Our souls may be revived, but that should spill over into mission. It bears fruit. It's not just for us, but the revival was also meant for all around us. It's not just meant to connect with individual souls, but true revival also brings a change in our relationships, in our communities, and in our societies.

It breaks out into the world.

It really has to create a new normal, not only in us but around us: a new normal that is good and just.

And it's also personal. Some may take issue with our insistence that revival could actually be located in an individual's experience. Didn't we just spend a lot of time trying to say that revivals aren't just a blip on the screen, not just a one-time event? Yes, we still hold to that. They are not moments, but movements, and yet they often start in someone's soul.

Seminary professors Malcolm McDow and Alvin Reid put it this way: "Revivals always start with personal encounters with God and travel through concentric circles to their conclusions.... Revival always starts with that one or those few who are serious with God, are ignited by God, and who become flames from which others can be set afire." It's such a pattern that we can be confident enough to say this: no revival in history started without revived people. In a very real sense, revival starts within someone or a within a group of people.

Early twentieth century evangelist Rodney "Gypsy" Smith was once asked how to start a revival. He replied, "Go home. Lock yourself in your room. Kneel down in the middle of the floor, and with a piece of chalk draw a circle around yourself. There, on your knees, pray fervently and brokenly that God would start a revival within that chalk circle."

We can't ignore the personal experience of revival. It's a seed. It begins small and unnoticed in the soil of a desperate heart, but can also escalate into a people movement that spreads its branches broadly enough so that communities and even nations may find refuge in them.

Levels of Revival

Revivals can be like earthquakes. With the seismograph, scientists can both detect and measure an earthquake. But not all earthquakes are the same. We live in Southern California, so unfortunately, we know earthquakes. Some shake while others roll. Some feel like a sudden drop while others swish around a bit. To measure an earthquake's magnitude, scientists use the Richter scale.

What's interesting about the Richter scale is that no matter where the tremors register—whether at a 1.0 or a 9.0—they're all earthquakes. Some make the six o'clock news while others don't disturb our slumber, but these earthquakes are happening every day, every hour, all over the world.

In this way, we plot revivals on a chart of ranging magnitude, indicating their breadth and depth of impact on a 1-5 scale:

Level one: Personal revivals. At this level, the revival dynamic is localized to an individual. Renewed intimacy with God, where heart and mind are electrified by the nearness of his presence, is the burning center of the moment. Scripture, prayer, and worship come alive with holy expectancy. With this newfound intimacy with God, new light is cast on the assumptions and paradigms of the day. As a result, questions around topics left untouched by the prevailing church culture rise to the surface for biblical engagement, such as the nature of the gospel, the experimentation with the gifts of the Spirit, or the need for social reform and engagement with the marginalized and neglected.

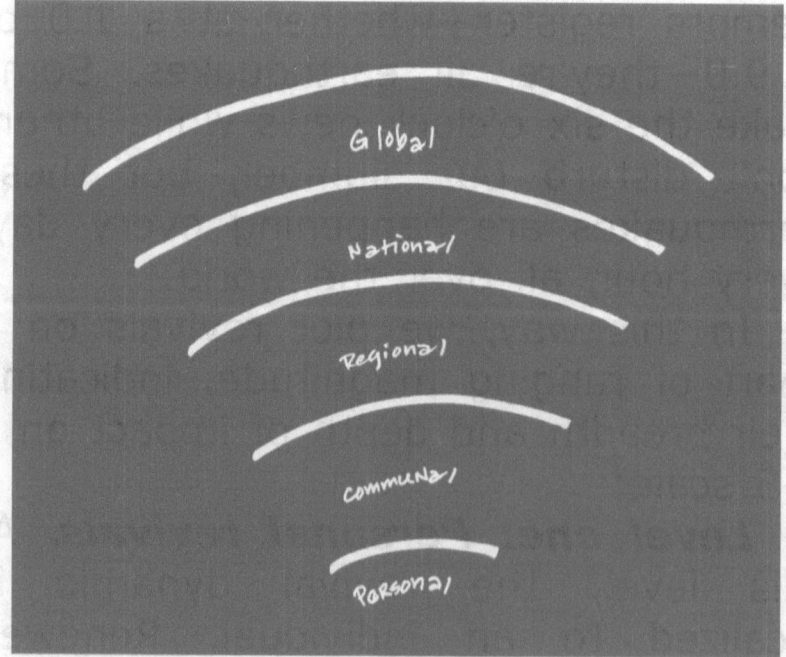

Figure 2. Levels of revival

Level two: Communal revivals. The influence of the personal revival begins to spread to the larger community, permeating the broader network of relationships with a small group, campus fellowship, local church, school, business, or other organization. Or perhaps the revival starts here because a group of people experienced a move of God together. At this level, enthusiasm is growing, but so is apprehension. At the personal level, other people choose whether to participate. But as the revival dynamic engages the broader community, it becomes unavoidable for those who are uncomfortable with the changes in the status quo. Wise and humble leadership at this stage is critical to mitigate division and distrust.

Level three: Regional revivals. Revival starts to transform a city or region across denominational, racial, and socioeconomic boundaries. Word of mouth spreads awareness of this new thing well beyond the point of conception. As more people catch the wind of inspiration generated by the movement, new voices are added to the mix, some for the better and some for the worse, and the movement either grows through the synergy or dissipates from the confusion. Every revival movement, as a challenge to the status quo, is marked by some level of controversy. But at this stage, tensions reach critical levels because heresy and confusion find their greatest opportunity. Many have a knee-jerk, defensive reaction against this new work of God.

Level four: National revivals. The dynamics of the local revival spread across the country, affecting society at institutional and systemic levels. The impact on individual lives disrupts entrenched cultural paradigms and practices. Cultural norms begin to be upended, and societal injustices start to be addressed. Media outlets begin to report on movements at this level, fueling debate and discussion.

Level five: Global revivals. This level is closely aligned with the previous one. When a revival reaches national magnitude, it tends also to have a ripple effect globally. It quickly moves beyond national boundaries, as people come to witness the revival, or others are sent to share the message.

In 1738, John Wesley, having failed in his mission to the American South, sailed back to England with uncertainty about his calling and doubts about his relationship with God. After a series of heart-searching meetings with Moravian leader Peter Boehler, he made his way to Aldersgate Street. There, a personal breakthrough sparked a level-one revival in the plowed soil of Wesley's soul:

> In the evening, I went very unwillingly to a society in Aldersgate Street, where one was reading Luther's preface to the Epistle to the Romans. About a quarter before nine, while he was describing the change which God works in the heart through faith in Christ, I felt my heart strangely warmed. I felt I did trust in Christ, Christ alone for salvation, and an assurance was given me that he had taken away my sins, even mine, and saved me from the law of sin and death.

The impact of this moment, though profoundly personal, would not remain private. Inspired by the example of the

Moravian prayer vigil, Wesley gathered others, including his brother Charles Wesley and George Whitefield, to commit themselves to seeking God for a greater outpouring of the Spirit. On January 1, 1739, eight months after Wesley's Aldersgate encounter, a level-two revival ignited as more than sixty people in Wesley's network of relationships felt their hearts warmed as well: "About three in the morning, as we were continuing instant in prayer, the power of God came mightily upon us, insomuch that many cried out for exceeding joy, and many fell to the ground."

Within weeks of this prayer meeting, the revival expanded to level three when George Whitefield led a preaching campaign in Bristol. Although it started small, it quickly exploded to crowds of thousands. Within four days, over ten thousand people crowded in daily to hear Whitefield's open-air preaching. Before long, he brought in John Wesley to help, and in the rush of excitement, boldly predicted, "The fire is kindled in the country; and I know, all the devils in hell shall not be able to quench it."

Testimonies spread through word of mouth, inspiring others to take up the call to spread the fire. Wesley and the Methodists escalated the revival to a level-four national phenomenon. Whitefield was a fantastic preacher, but John Wesley's organizational skill conserved the revival's wild energy from dissipating and being lost. Organizing people into bands, classes, and societies to disciple new believers channeled the revival into the untouched relational networks of the newly converted.

As the level-four revival went on, its impact on English society was dramatic. John Wesley encouraged Christians to seek social reform. He personally gave away all his writing profits to the poor. He spoke out vehemently against the slave trade and encouraged William Wilberforce in his antislavery efforts. And the Methodists and other Christian communities continued to serve others in exceptional ways. In describing their impact, the historian Diane Severance writes:

> Numerous agencies promoting Christian work arose as a result of the eighteenth-century revival in

England. Antislavery societies, prison reform groups, and relief agencies for the poor were started. Numerous missionary societies were formed; the Religious Tract Society was organized; and the British Foreign Bible Society was established. Hospitals and schools multiplied. The revival cut across denominational lines and touched every class of society. England itself was transformed by the revival.

It didn't stop there. Refusing to be quenched by the miles of ocean waters, the revival crossed the Atlantic and set North America ablaze as well. Like a burning ember, Whitefield joined what God was already doing through many others such as William Tennent and Jonathan Edwards, and continued to spark revival after revival in almost every town he visited. The First Great Awakening matured to a level-five global awakening.

Revival and the Kingdom of God

Where revivals break through, so does the kingdom of God. In the Gospels, Jesus proclaimed that the kingdom of God was near. It's where God's will is fulfilled on earth, where heaven breaks through, and all of its resources are available to us. It's where what God wants to happen, actually happens. This breakthrough is not something we can force or schedule, but it's glorious when it shows up. And revivals are one of the most visible ways where the kingdom of God is made evident.

Revivals are an obvious expression of heaven touching earth.

Jesus taught us to pray, "Your kingdom come, your will be done, on earth as it is in heaven." In teaching us to pray in this way, Jesus gave us the seed of a much larger reality. Thoughts and prayers always have within them a potential to escalate into so much more, if they are given a chance to mature and be lived out.

Perhaps this is something of what Jesus was hinting at when he talked about the kingdom of God being like a mustard seed—something that is small at first but can eventually grow into something so much bigger.

And he lived it out. Jesus lived a revived life. More than anyone before or after him. He declared that in his single life, the kingdom of God had come near. Jesus, the king, was present. Something much bigger had begun.

Heaven broke through.

And from one life, a moment on the cross transformed into a movement of shalom and salvation that encompassed the entire world. Seasons of breakthroughs—in word, deed, and power—created a new normal, and the world has never been the same.

Discussion Questions

1. What part of the definition of revival stood out to you? Why?
2. If you were to place a dot that best represents your faith expression on Figure 1, "The full

proclamation of the gospel," where would you put yourself? In what ways is God inviting you more to the center?
3. What level of revival have you been a part of? What was that like?

Chapter Two

FROM HOLY DISCONTENT TO CRUCIFIED HOPE

Hope is a function of struggle.
BRENÉ BROWN, *DARING GREATLY*

Whoever wants to be my disciple must deny themselves and take up their cross daily and follow me.
JESUS OF NAZARETH, LUKE 9:23

It was late into an August night when a hand on my shoulder gently shook me from my sleep. My eyes blinked, trying to focus on the figure silhouetted by the hallway light.

"Ryan," he whispered. "Please wake up. I need you to talk to me about Jesus."

I sat straight up and immediately turned on the light. What did he just say? Wasn't this the guy who had sternly warned me all those years ago never to tell him about Jesus?

"What's up, Dad? Are you okay?"

It was the best I had at the moment.

His face was pale, and his eyes moved around wildly, searching for something. I actually wondered if he was having a heart attack.

"Son, I've mocked you and God for these past six years. I'm not mocking you anymore. Please tell me about Jesus."

What welled up within me wasn't a gale of courage or boldness. Instead, I froze in fear and insecurity. How could I lead my dad to faith? I was just a college kid. Why not put a scalpel in my hand and ask me to perform surgery?

With a quick prayer under my breath, I asked my dad some questions to understand the details of his spiritual crisis. Ultimately, he wanted peace with God. Three hours passed, and with each word I offered about the good news of Jesus, more courage broke through. Hope began to rise. And it seemed that every prayer spoken through all those long years was about to be fulfilled.

Then it happened. He lifted his hands to heaven. Tears streamed down his face. He followed my lead in prayer.

He confessed his sin. He asked for forgiveness.

He gave his life to Jesus.

I told him that the Holy Spirit would come to live inside of him and prayed that God would give him some sign of the Spirit's filling.

My dad looked up. He was radiant. Years of grief had fallen from my dad's face. Then he explained that a warm, burning sensation was working its way up from his feet, through his chest, to the top of his head.

"I feel like I'm being filled with liquid fire," he said. "And I feel a peace I've never felt before."

"That sounds like the Holy Spirit to me, Dad."

The Breakthrough U Curve

At my bedside that night, God broke through. But it took six years. Ever since I became a Christian, I wanted my dad to give himself to Jesus' great love and leadership.

So why did it take so long?

If God has the power to change my dad's heart, why didn't he just do it right away? Why make me wait? If there's a purpose to the waiting, how should I deal with the time in-between?

We could turn to the Bible and ask similar questions: Why did the Israelites have to wait for hundreds of years in Egyptian slavery before God sent Moses to deliver them? Why did Jesus wait two more days before going to raise Lazarus back to life? Why did Jesus have to die and descend for three days before he could rise and reign?

Biblical prayers have been written with this in mind. For example:
> How long, Lord? Will you forget me forever?
> How long will you hide your face from me?
> How long must I wrestle with my thoughts and day after day have sorrow in my heart?
> How long will my enemy triumph over me?

We don't know the mind of God, so we can't offer any specific answers about what you're going through or waiting for. But when it comes to revival, breakthrough is an essential concept to understand. We're not talking about a flash-in-the-pan spirituality that seeks shortcuts and quick fixes. Nor are we saying that God will tick off every item on your prayer list in the way you envision it.

But in every revival, by definition, there is a season of breakthrough. And breakthrough assumes a struggle, a need for endurance, a season of waiting.

After studying dozens of biblical examples as well as historical ones, we began to see that the process of breakthrough took on a certain shape. We're calling it the breakthrough U curve. We know that we can't make revival happen; only God can do that. But our hope is that this paradigm will help you find your latitude and longitude on the big map of your journey toward kingdom breakthrough, and offer some much-needed perspective to help you endure the waiting with hope and expectancy.

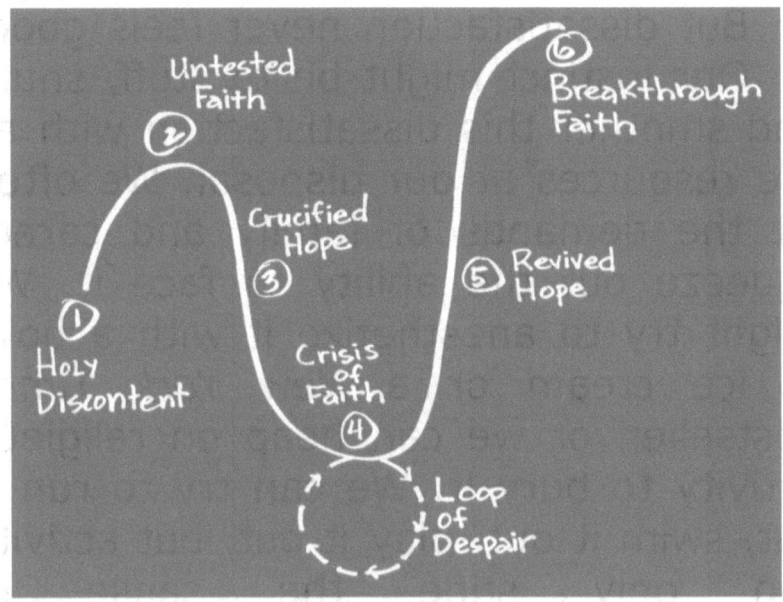

Figure 3. Breakthrough U curve

Stage One: Holy Discontent

Breakthrough typically begins with dissatisfaction with the status quo. What we've previously accepted as unchangeable, permanent, or permissible starts to give way to longing for something better. We start asking, Does it really have to be this way? Is this what God has in mind for me, my family, our church, our campus, and our culture? Is this what my life is going to end up looking like? Is this who I really want to be?

But dissatisfaction never feels good.

Our instinct might be to stuff, snuff, and smother this dissatisfaction with all the resources at our disposal. We often let the demands of family and career squeeze out the ability to face it. We might try to anesthetize it with a bowl of ice cream or a *New York Times* bestseller, or we can heap on religious activity to bury it. We can try to run it out, swim it out, play it out, but activity can only stifle the sense of dissatisfaction for so long.

When I (Ryan) first became a Christian, it started to dawn on me that my parents did not have a saving faith in Jesus. They were so uncomfortable with my best friend who had led me to faith that they barred him from our house and required that I end the friendship. They tried to dissuade me from my newfound faith with vague notions of reincarnation, personal power, and self-help.

When talking about me, the word *fanatic* was thrown around a lot.

At first, these conversations frustrated and angered me. How could my parents believe all that New Age stuff? I thought we were Christian: we went to church on holidays, and they had me baptized, confirmed, and sent me to catechism classes. Then it began to sink in. Even with the upbringing and ritual, maybe they didn't have a saving relationship with Jesus.

That realization was hard to swallow. If I embraced it fully, then the status quo was over. My parents were no longer just good people, and their relationship with God—or lack thereof—could no longer be ignored. Embracing the discontent meant facing a problem that was bigger than I could solve and raising questions I was afraid to answer: Are my parents saved? Could they end up separated from God for eternity? The questions made me squirm.

Dissatisfaction, however, is a powerful, disruptive—even needed—force that can awaken our soul to God's desires. Jesus called the dissatisfied, blessed: "Blessed are the poor in spirit, ... blessed are those who mourn, ...

blessed are those who hunger and thirst for righteousness, ... blessed are the peacemakers." The discontent want something they do not yet have, and in that tension, Jesus called them blessed. Deep in their longings is the beginning of breakthrough. Far from breaking us down, this discontent holds the first key to breakthrough in our lives.

People who seek revival begin by finding their holy discontent.

Author John Eldredge wrote: "Christianity has nothing to say to the person who is completely happy with the way things are. Its message is for those who hunger and thirst—for those who desire life as it was meant to be." Throughout our lives, the Holy Spirit seeks to use the disappointments, failures, losses, and heartaches to awaken us to this desire for life as it was meant to be. As my pastor often puts it, "Don't waste your pain."

God is able to take desires—like your longing to have a baby or your anger with the suffering in the world—and make them work for good. With our heart in God's hands, he helps us get to the bottom of our discontent, and he performs the alchemy of transforming our dissatisfaction into godly desires. This in turn produces energy that empowers us to take bold action: to take a stand in the face of injustice, to speak up for the disadvantaged, to make radical life changes for a cause that pays less but promises more, to pray with a conviction that brings us to the very heart of God.

Jesus provoked this kind of holy longing in Peter. Early in the Gospels, Peter, a fisherman, was tired after a long, fruitless night on the Sea of Galilee. He had only empty nets to carry back to shore for cleaning. Instead of a much-needed rest, he found himself pushing back out to sea because Jesus chose to use his boat as a pulpit. To make matters worse, Jesus, after his teaching, insisted that Peter push out into deeper water and lower his nets yet again.

A subtle pressure on the lines quickly avalanched into a full-blown tug of war with what seemed to be every fish in the sea. With the small boat sinking under the sheer weight of the overflowing nets, Peter strained to pull aboard the catch of a lifetime. In the middle of the excitement, Peter's attention shifted away from the catch to the silent, intense gaze of Jesus.

Peter gets it. "Master, leave. I'm a sinner and can't handle this holiness. Leave me to myself."

Jesus' reply was even more startling. "There is nothing to fear. From now on you'll be fishing for men and women."

Jesus gave Peter what he had dreamed of—the best catch of his career—and then goaded him with an invitation to follow him. It's as if he's saying, "Is this all you want? What if I have something even better? You now have what you've always wanted, but I know you hunger for more. Don't be afraid of it; embrace it."

Jesus' invitation forced Peter to be honest about what he really wanted. Did he want the most lucrative fishing career in Galilee or the chance to catch human lives with the love of God?

In the same way, people who seek revival are honest about their heart's desires and offer them to God so that the Spirit can teach them to hunger and thirst for God's kingdom. The Spirit uses these awakened desires like bread crumbs to lead us to bigger breakthroughs. We must learn to hunger and thirst for God's help, growing in confidence that he is faithful to give us something more.

Let's not be afraid of the longings that are being stirred in us. Instead, take them to God. Some of us have been disappointed before and are afraid history will repeat itself. Others of us might worry that confronting our discontent will only lead to discouragement, frustration, or even anger. A few of us might be afraid to fan the flame in others, just in case we're accused of burning down the house with emotionalism or fanaticism.

Faith, however, is not about suppressing our desires so that things don't get out of hand. Isn't it about allowing the Spirit to awaken the desires God has planted within us through the indwelling of his Spirit and his Word?

Using this very idea, Spurgeon counsels us about prayer that breaks through: "Do not ask for what some tell you that you should ask for, but for that which you feel the need of, that which the Holy Spirit has made you to hunger and to thirst for, you ask for that." Notice how he moves seamlessly from "that which you feel the need of" right into, "that which the Holy Spirit has made you to hunger and to thirst for."

In the first stage of the breakthrough U curve (figure 3), we allow the Spirit to revive in us the Father's desires already planted within our hearts. Eldredge writes something along similar lines: "When transformation comes, it is always the aftereffect of something else, something at the level of our hearts. At its core, Christianity begins with an invitation to desire."

The journey of seeking God for revival begins with an invitation to desire. If we were not afraid, what would we seek? Where is God stirring discontent in our lives? Where do we long for change in the status quo? It doesn't have to be overtly spiritual, like wanting to see our families fall in love with Jesus. The key thing here is that it's personal and grabs us in the gut, even if it seems like an unspiritual desire at first.

In other words, where do you feel the strongest desire for change? Is it in your marriage, in your health, in your womb, in your finances, in your community, in racial dynamics, in politics, in your country, or in the world? Nothing is off-limits to the Holy Spirit. And we trust the Holy Spirit to lead us back—even if it changes from what we initially hoped for—into his desires and will.

Jesus had once asked: "What do you want me to do for you?" When we're ready to answer that question honestly, then we're ready for the next stage of breakthrough.

Stage Two: Untested Faith

Wanting something, however, can only take us so far. Wanting doesn't give us the confidence to know that our desires are aligned with the kingdom of God. What we need now is for God to begin speaking into the discontent. In stage two, faith gets its first intake of breath toward breakthrough.

With my (Ryan's) family, a passion for their salvation inspired conversations about Jesus, yet it also produced tense arguments and broken trust. A growing sense of failure and discouragement threatened my newfound zeal.

Thumbing through my Bible for inspiration, I stumbled upon Jesus' encounter with Zacchaeus. Jesus told him, "Today salvation has come to this house, because this man, too, is a son of Abraham. For the Son of Man came to seek and to save the lost." Zacchaeus's searching not only brought salvation to his life but also to his whole household.

This passage stirred up a vague memory of another part of Scripture. I found myself turning to Acts 16 where Paul and Silas led the jailer to faith: "'Sirs, what must I do to be saved?' They replied, 'Believe in the Lord Jesus, and you will be saved—you and your household.'"

You and your household. Those last four words jumped off the page right into my soul. Jesus doesn't just save individuals, he saves families. He doesn't just save a person, he saves communities. It's a pattern in God's kingdom: Cornelius's, Lydia's, and Crispus's households in the Bible came to faith as a unit, right? For me, my conversion was a sign that God had intentions to save the rest of my family.

I was the first fruit of God's larger plan.

Through Scripture, my desire turned to faith. I was no longer afraid. I was expectant. This newfound confidence in Jesus filled me with joy and excitement. As a result, I argued less and listened more with my parents. Instead of trying to resolve my worry in pointless debates, I poured out my heart to God in prayer, knowing that he was the one I needed to talk to the most.

Bringing our desires to God's Word allows the Spirit to align our hearts with God's promises. Raw passion is never enough to carry us to kingdom breakthrough; we need the enduring strength of faith that comes from God's Word. True faith draws its power from trusting God's loyalty to his promise in our particular situations and circumstances as well as his track record of faithfulness in our lives.

On the breakthrough U curve (figure 3), this stage is represented by a positive bump on the graph because of the increase of confidence and expectation this new faith brings with it. Untested faith, even in this fledgling form, is still the beginning of real faith. Faith is truly given. We find ourselves able to trust in God's character and intention as it applies to our situation.

It would be tempting to disparage the faith we see at this point. It's just emotions. It hasn't been tested. But that doesn't make it any less real. It's not fools' gold—it just hasn't yet matured.

It's the honeymoon.

Zechariah exhorts us, "Do not despise these small beginnings." It's a time of excitement and hope—don't take that away from yourself or others. Untested faith contains the raw elements that can blossom into great faith, even breakthrough faith. Sure, it needs discipline and refinement. Dross also needs to be burned away. Let's not discourage it but instead affirm it, nurture it, and guide it along to maturity.

Peter found himself in the euphoria of this early stage. Jesus had initiated a conversation about his identity, and Peter responded with sharp accuracy: Jesus is Messiah, the Son of the living God. It was a clear, unequivocal confirmation about who Jesus really is, and Jesus responds to Peter with enthusiasm and blessing:

> Blessed are you, Simon son of Jonah, for this was not revealed to you by flesh and blood, but by my Father in heaven.... You are Peter, and on this rock I will build my church, and the gates of Hades will not overcome it. I will give you the keys of the kingdom of heaven; whatever you bind on earth will be bound in heaven, and whatever you loose on earth will be loosed in heaven.

Jesus doesn't quench this early spark of faith. He knows that Peter's faith will be tested from this point on, yet this marks the beginning of something more.

Nevertheless, faith at this stage is untested. False expectations about the timing, method, or process worm their way in. Selfish ambitions cloud reality. Foundations are weak, and we must be tested and refined in the stages to come if this upstart faith is to mature and become effective in God's kingdom.

We do need to be gracious with ourselves and others at this stage. At a wedding between a young bride and groom, we don't sit at the back table with our arms folded thinking, *They have no idea what they're getting into. How can they be so happy, when they know it's going to be such hard work?* Sure, marriages require hard work, but to be scornful and pessimistic at the wedding would be deeply cynical. Instead, we rightfully celebrate the stage they are at, and perhaps something in our own heart is softened by their youthful wonder and passion.

The joy and energy of this stage has an important place in the process. It's meant to fill us with celebration and thanksgiving because God is on the move.

Stage Three: Crucified Hope

Still, for faith to mature, our hope often gets crucified. The first blush of excitement gives way to a major obstacle or failure. The seedling seems stuck in the ground. In this stage, the rubber of our faith truly meets the road.

I (Ryan) am the oldest in a family of five children. I started to follow Jesus first but led my brother Eric to faith. Together, we prayed often for our dad to come to faith. We reasoned that if he gave his life to Jesus, as impossible as that seemed at the time, it would convince the rest of the family that Jesus was real.

On the night my dad came to faith, I ran outside the house to find Eric praying on the front curb. He had been praying during the entire three-hour conversation. With my hands raised above my head in triumph, I shouted, "Dad has accepted Jesus!" My brother jumped up, and with a running start, joy-tackled me to the pavement of our driveway.

Momentum was rising. With Dad on our side, I felt certain the rest of the family, like dominoes in quick succession, would quickly follow his lead.

Instead, my parents got divorced.

Despite their best efforts to protect the rest of the family, we all felt terrible confusion and pain from the breakdown of our family. My dad's conversion didn't bring my parents closer together as I had hoped. Instead, it pushed them further apart.

It was hard to reconcile what I'd heard from God years before—that he would save my entire family—with what was unfolding before me. I found myself asking familiar questions, "God, where are you? What happened to the faith and vision you gave me for my family's salvation? Why are you letting us get torn apart? Why are you letting this happen to us?"

When I turned to God in prayer, I heard him tell me difficult things that I didn't want to hear such as, "Your family is going to die, but I will bring them new life." I found no comfort in this. I didn't want my family to fall apart. This was not the way it was supposed to go. My expectations were crucified.

Sliding toward the bottom of the breakthrough U curve is where we find stage three—crucified hope. It's where hope is dashed against the rocks, and all the pieces lie scattered on the ground. The excitement of faith fades into the backdrop of reality. Life is hard. Faith is tested. The downward descent of the U curve represents the death of false hopes and false expectations that we have carried into the journey. This is where God purifies our faith in the refiner's fire, because it's hard to trust God when he doesn't do things the way we imagined.

Coming back to Peter, he had faith that Jesus was Messiah, but it was on his own terms. Immediately after he encouraged Peter, Jesus shared that he would have to suffer, be killed, and be raised to life on the third day. This came into sharp conflict with Peter's expectations, so much so that he rebuked Jesus for saying these things.

Jesus responded even more harshly: "Get behind me, Satan! You are a stumbling block to me; you do not have in mind the concerns of God, but merely human concerns." Jesus had just blessed him moments ago; now he gave Peter a stinging rebuke. Peter must've felt shock, shame, and confusion as the deep dread of death began to cast its shadow over his hopes.

Before breakthrough, our expectations are crucified, so we've labeled this stage crucified hope for three reasons. First, crucifixion is about dying. False ideas we have about God must die. At an even deeper level, our sins must also be crucified. Our pride and self-reliance must be put to death, otherwise we remain deceived by the lie that revival is within our ability or resources. We kill expectations so Jesus can lead us to greater things.

Second, crucifixion is slow. The process of crucifixion was not only intense and difficult, but it was painstakingly drawn out. The victim didn't hang for hours but for days before his death. In the same way, waiting is another way to die to ourselves. The longer we have to wait on God to fulfill his promise, the more we die to ourselves and the more our true colors show.

The waiting exposes our false expectations and hopes. In the days of instant information, we'll be tempted to short-circuit this process. We'll want to give up on God, bail, and move on to the next thing. Don't. Waiting is an essential but often forgotten spiritual practice. In fact, "to hope" and "to wait" in the Old Testament are actually translated from the same Hebrew word.

If every promise were followed by an immediate fulfillment, there would be no waiting, and therefore there would be no need for hoping. Paul, with his Hebrew worldview, understood this when he wrote, "Hope that is seen is no hope at all. Who hopes for what they already have? But if we hope for what we do not yet have, we wait for it patiently." Waiting and hoping are inseparably intertwined.

In this way, the waiting exposes our dependence on emotions. In our untested faith, it's easy to confuse confidence with positive feelings. Although faith can be expressed with emotion, it can't be defined by it. So the Spirit exposes our faith's weak foundations, only to anchor it in the ground of God's promises and character instead.

Third, although crucified, there is still hope. False hopes have been crucified so that true hope can be revived. False expectations have been laid bare so that a holy expectancy can be embraced. We've come face-to-face with hopes that were never meant to give us true hope in the first place, and we're more sober minded and clear headed about what grounds us. Our feet have come back from the heavens and find themselves planted back on earth.

The great discovery of this stage is that the death of our false hopes doesn't result in the death of our faith. Although it is painful to have our false expectations shattered in front of our eyes, we need to guard ourselves and each other from losing faith. It's far too easy to feel played like the fool.

But take heart. When God doesn't work on our terms, the only thing dying is our will, not God's. And although this knowledge doesn't take the sting out of the process, it can keep us from despair and giving up.

But it usually gets worse before it gets better.

Discussion Questions

1. In this season, what do you really want God to do for you? What do you sense God calling you to do?
2. In what ways have things not gone as planned or hoped?
3. How is God asking you to wait on him in this season?

Chapter Three

FROM CRISIS OF FAITH TO BREAKTHROUGH FAITH

Again and again the history of revival has been the history of God's intervention to retrieve what was hopeless.
ARTHUR WALLIS, *IN THE DAY OF THY POWER*

Against all hope, Abraham in hope believed.
PAUL OF TARSUS, ROMANS 4:18

As we head into the final three stages, the breakthrough U curve doesn't yet turn upward. It actually slips further to its nadir, and here the Spirit leads us to a choice: Will we surrender false hopes and the lies we believed so we can find our hope in God alone, or will we cling to our false hopes and allow them to drag us into despair?

Stage Four: Crisis of Faith

In this stage, a sense of crisis begins to overtake us. We can be more vulnerable to despair and are increasingly tempted to give up. Our strength and resources are simply not enough to produce the results we hoped for. The light at the end of the tunnel has stopped glimmering, and our repeated efforts have failed. Others, with deep concern, counsel us to move on and accept "God's will."

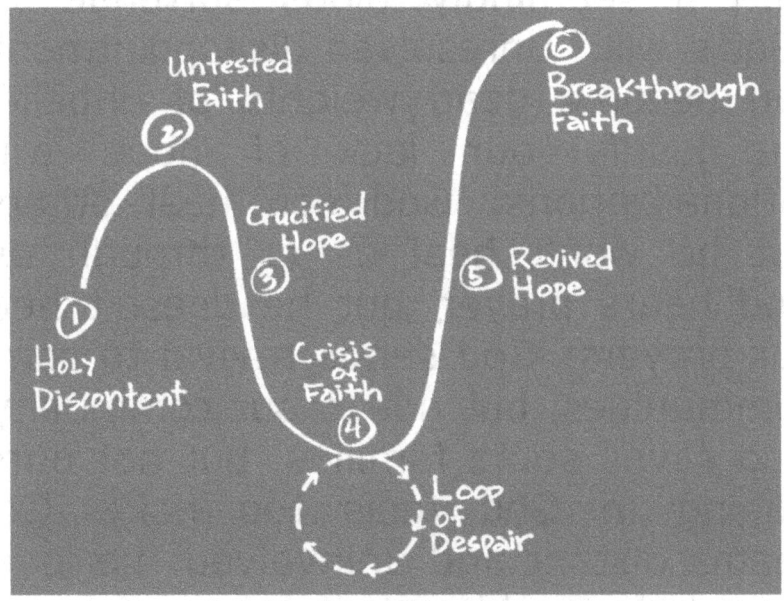

Figure 4. Breakthrough U curve

We stand on the brink of total discouragement and disengagement.

The entire breakthrough process hinges on this stage. It's good to let go of something because it was never a promise from God to begin with. Letting go, however, of a longing for breakthrough simply because we can't imagine it anymore—that is a breakdown in faith altogether.

In a way, stage four is a crossroads, a choice between two paths.

The loop of despair. On one path, we can choose to give up hope in God and cover up the longings of our heart with a seemingly pious surrender to "God's will." Unresolved disappointments can become dead weights of unbelief. We justify our lack of hope with rationalizations: God can heal others, but he won't heal us or through us; God hears prayer, but he doesn't hear our prayers; God sends revival to some communities, but not to our community; God saves some families, but not ours. Hoping in God feels too risky. God seems distant and uninvolved: he loves the whole world except me.

This choice leads us into the downward spiral of the loop of despair. It becomes a kind of purgatory, holding us captive until we confront the lies behind our disappointment.

Kristina, a friend and colleague of ours, had been asking God to give her the gift of healing. When asked by a student if Jesus still heals today, she didn't hesitate to say in faith, "Yes!" So he asked her to come pray for his seventeen-year-old brother, who was dying in a hospital bed. Certain of God's leading, she agreed. She felt both nervous and confident that God would move miraculously through her.

But within a couple of days, Kristina heard that he had died.

Devastated by the news, Kristina vowed never to pray for anyone to be healed again. Incriminating questions beat in her mind like jungle drums: *Who was I to think God could use me? All I did was make things worse for that family. I was so stupid for thinking God was going to heal that guy.*

She had spiraled into the loop of despair. It's like being stuck in a hamster wheel, running trapped in a cycle of unbelief fed by disillusionment, confusion, and torment. We might know friends who've been caught in this cycle for decades, enslaved by the pain of past failures and losses.

But there is a way out.

The path to breakthrough. In the path to breakthrough, we realize that we never had the strength or resources on our own to fulfill God's promises. We accept that we are prone to place expectations on God's promises that he never himself encouraged, and we ask him to free us from them. We allow God to revive our hope in him out of the ashes of the dead hope in ourselves. This is where we choose to face the brutal facts of our complete and total inadequacy to fulfill God's promises, to produce God's breakthrough, or to usher in God's revival.

We let our expectations die and embrace expectancy.

There's a difference between expectations and expectancy. Expectations demand a certain result; expectancy trusts and hopes. Expectations create anger and disillusionment in our faith when they aren't met; expectancy is an openness to any outcome God desires. Expectations force God into a box to act as we want; expectancy allows God to be God in our lives, acting on his own will. Broken expectations, on their own, lead us to despair; expectancy takes our broken expectations back to God to rebuild our faith. The crisis gives us an opportunity to relinquish our expectations so that expectancy can grow in our soul.

We've heard it said, "Expectations are resentments under construction." We need to kill our expectations or they will kill our faith.

The choice toward expectancy, however, transforms us. We are liberated from the deception of false hope to find a resurrection waiting for us in a revived hope in God. We give up on ourselves; we give up on our circumstances to tell us what is possible. We even give up, if needed, on the encouragement of others to reassure us. We don't know how God will do it, we don't know when God will do it, but we have made a choice: to trust that God is able to do all that he has promised, and to leave the results to him. We kill our expectations but raise expectancy.

Moving forward in Peter's story, nothing had turned out as he had expected. It was the third time he had heard the rooster's crow. It meant nothing to everyone else around the fire ring, but the sound stabbed his heart. Jesus had predicted it. An avalanche of shock and horror fell on him: he had failed Jesus.

He swore he wouldn't—upon his life!—but he had. Overwhelmed with shame, he fled into the shadows of the surrounding trees to be alone. I imagine self-recrimination swarmed his thoughts: *How could I fail him? Didn't I try and fight for him with sword in hand? Didn't I try and follow if even from a distance? Didn't I vow to him, though everyone abandoned him, I never would, that, "I am ready to go with you to prison and to death"?*

This moment of crisis placed Peter on a dangerous precipice. Everything had been stripped from him. All his faith in himself had finally been broken.

Peter must've felt as if his options were miserable: Would he, like Judas, take his own life? Or smeared with the stain of his failure, would he abandon the disciples and go into exile? And once Jesus was crucified, what then? Jesus had failed to fulfill all their expectations. Nothing had turned out as they had hoped and prayed, only as they had feared.

Which path would Peter choose?

It's a choice we often have to make as well. Who gets to be in control? Will we completely surrender to God?

Surrender is the essential posture.

After my parents' divorce, I told my therapist that I was moving home. I couldn't bear to watch my family suffer from a distance. My plan: I'd quit doing campus ministry in San Diego and move back to Orange County. How could I sit in San Diego while my family needed me?

My therapist paused for a moment before asking, "Ryan, where is Jesus in this family crisis?"

I resented the question. More accurately, the question exposed my resentment. "I don't know! I don't see him anywhere!"

"Can we pray and ask Jesus to show you where he is in all of this?"

I reluctantly closed my eyes, asking Jesus to show me where he was. I could feel my anger welling up inside along with the doubt that anything meaningful would happen.

I expected to see nothing. But as I prayed, an image slowly came into focus. I could see a dense, dark fog in front of me, and from behind me, one by one, my family members were walking past me into the fog and disappearing. When I saw my little eleven-year-old sister, Alysa, walk into the fog, I chased after her, only to get lost inside.

Gently but resolutely, my therapist probed, "And where is Jesus?"

"I don't know!" I snapped back. "He's nowhere! He's abandoned us! I don't see him!"

"Ask Jesus again to show you where he is."

This time, there was no delay. Fog enveloped my family, and I ran in after them just as before. This time, however, Jesus was standing in front of me, blocking my path.

"Get out of my way Jesus! You're not doing anything! Someone has to do something!"

Tears streamed down my face, and my body shook as I tried to hold back the full force of my emotions. But Jesus bent down—because in this scene, I'm small as a child—and as he reached my eye level, I could see that he knew my pain.

"Ryan, this is my job, not yours. Trust me."

With that, he stood up, turned, and disappeared into the fog to get my family.

I finally understood that my going home wasn't out of faith but instead out of fear and self-determination. Like Peter, I had taken up my sword. I would fight to save my family. And in truth, I had been fighting this way for months, but my best efforts made a bigger mess with every visit home.

I had to make a choice. Would I let my own hopes and plans for my family die and trust that Jesus could save them his way, or would I give up my faith in Jesus' promise altogether and shoulder the burden on my own? Would I surrender my plans in order to discover God's?

Stage Five: Revived Hope

If we haven't slipped off the U curve into the loop of despair, then we've done the work of basing our hope not in what we can understand, explain, or strategize. We are starting to climb the U curve again with renewed expectancy into stage five: revived hope.

For Peter, the women's story was too good to be true. They had burst into the room with a glint in their eyes, mouthing the impossible: Jesus is alive! In response, most of the disciples hedged, held back, guarded their hearts, and shook their heads at the utter nonsense of it all.

Hope, after all, is a dangerous thing.

But Peter had gone lower than anyone else into the abyss of crucified hope; he had denied Jesus three times, losing hope in himself three times over. Perhaps that's why Peter was the first to jump up and run to the tomb. He had a hope against all hope that Jesus had done what he had promised.

Revived hope is where you haven't yet seen the fulfillment of God's promises but still find fresh expectancy in who God is. Peter faced his crisis of faith, but he didn't hang himself like Judas, he didn't abandon the community, he didn't run into shamed exile, nor did he dismiss the hope the women brought. He had no answers, no solutions, no strategies, and most of all, no hope in himself. His hope had been crucified. Yet as he ran, his hope was renewed.

When we've surrendered ourselves, our resources, and our circumstances, an internal breakthrough happens. A quiet resolve replaces the ups and downs of the previous stages; it's the calm after the storm. We become like Abraham, who "against all hope ... in hope believed.... He faced the fact that his body was as good as dead—since he was about a hundred years old—and that Sarah's womb was also dead." Abraham had to surrender his hope in his body and Sarah's womb, and place his hope in God alone.

We've killed expectations and have embraced expectancy that God will move.

But this stage, even in its newfound groundedness, is an emotionally vulnerable place to be. Brené Brown explains vulnerability as "uncertainty, risk, and emotional exposure." More reasonable voices want to caution us here: "Be careful. Don't get your hopes up." These voices quote Scripture to us: remember to "guard your heart." We are emotionally exposed when we hope against hope. We don't want to end up the fool.

But while untested faith might look like bravado, revived hope is an exercise in profound humility. True hope doesn't come from pretentious swagger or pompous boasting; instead it comes from a place of poverty and meekness. Preconceived expectations die. Expectancy rises again.

Back in my therapist's office, I was sitting with my eyes closed under his watchful gaze. In my mind's eye, Jesus disappeared into the fog to pursue my family. But then the scene shifted, and I saw his crucifixion. He hung on the cross, smeared in blood and agony. Yet he was resolute and determined to go into the deepest darkness.

I heard him say, "It is finished."

It's hard to convey the weight and force of what his words meant to me. I knew that it was not up to me to save my family anymore. A revived hope had somehow begun to shine in the shadows of my deepest doubts: Jesus would finish what he started. From that moment on, a growing hope was renewed in me, though I didn't know how or when or where he would do it. I was confident Jesus would break through even in the trauma of divorce.

It was clear now: moving home wasn't the solution. It was really a desperate idea driven by my fear and guilt. I gave up hope in my efforts, that I could save my family. I'd leave the saving to Jesus. Sure, I'd still go home on weekends and make calls to check up on my family. I'd keep praying. But the source of my hope wasn't in myself but in Jesus. My shoulders were unburdened. With trust in Jesus, I didn't move home.

Pastor John Piper, in describing the relationship between hope and faith, writes, "Hope is like a reservoir of emotional strength.... If I am put down, I look to the emotional reservoir of hope for the strength to return good for evil. Without hope I have no power to absorb the wrong and walk in love, and I sink into self-pity or self-justification."

Revived hope energizes our faith with fresh emotional strength. The reservoir of hope in God enlivens our faith with joy and assurance. Faith energized by hope is qualitatively different than faith that lacks hope. When we have hope, we don't need to have the answers to trust him. His promise and word are enough. Piper went on to write, "You might put it this way: faith is our confidence in the word of God, and whenever that word has reference to the future, you can call our confidence in it hope. Hope is faith in the future tense."

Hope is faith applied to the future. And with this new access to the deep reservoir of hope's emotional strength, we are launched upward into a rising faith for breakthrough.

Stage Six: Breakthrough Faith

In stage six, breakthrough finally happens. It might not have looked how we had originally thought, but an answer has finally broken through.

Recognizing the miracle. But ironically, this can be the most confusing stage of the entire process. It actually takes faith to believe good news, to hear the still, small voice, to see miracles, to receive breakthrough. Neither physical evidence nor concrete empirical data can substitute for it: faith enables us to see beneath the surface of things, to see the whole truth of a matter. We could be standing right in front of the breakthrough we have prayed for and longed for our whole lives and not even recognize it or receive it when it comes.

In other words, revival could be happening right before our eyes, but we might not have the faith to see it.

In Luke's twenty-fourth chapter, an odd encounter happened between two disciples and an unrecognizable Jesus. The author specifically states, "Jesus himself came up and walked along with them; but they were kept from recognizing him." It's an unbelievable scene where Cleopas and likely his wife found themselves walking with Jesus and even conversing about him without recognizing he was right there with them!

This scene makes me wonder at their inability to recognize him and even further what Luke means when he says they were kept from recognizing Jesus.

Luke won't let us off the hook yet, because in the next scene Jesus appears in the presence of all the disciples. Among others, the eleven apostles are in the room, minus the twelfth who betrayed him. Who would better recognize Jesus than them? Yet Luke gives us the painful truth: "They were startled and frightened, thinking they saw a ghost. He said to them, 'Why are you troubled, and why do doubts rise in your minds? Look at my hands and my feet. It is I myself! Touch me and see; a ghost does not have flesh and bones, as you see I have.'"

The story is familiar, but we need to marvel afresh at not only their inability to believe in Jesus—even if he's alive and well, eating a fish taco in front of them—but our inability to recognize God's breakthroughs even as they happen right in front of us.

Let's look more closely at how faith functions in this stage. In his book *The Knowledge of the Holy,* A.W. Tozer's description of faith helps us get to the heart of the problem. Tozer writes, "In Christ and by Christ, God effects complete self-disclosure, although he shows Himself not to reason but to faith and love. Faith is an organ of knowledge, and love an organ of experience."

Therefore, it's not by reason alone that you recognize the breakthrough—it's also by faith. Faith is what allows us to see what God is doing when it doesn't make sense to our reason, when it doesn't align with our expectations, and when it doesn't come in our timing. It simply wasn't reasonable to believe that Jesus had risen. Reason alone could not bridge the gulf of that contradiction, even with the empirical evidence standing right in front of them. We can't resolve these contradictions apart from faith. It's the reason that Jesus could do miracles and people still refused to believe in him.

Secondly, faith helps us switch gears in our thinking and feeling. We can get so comfortable in the waiting that the breakthrough of a new normal feels too disruptive to our status quo. It messes things up.

Think of how disruptive it was for Jesus to show up back in the beginning of the Gospel of Mark when he announced, "The time is fulfilled!" It meant the disciples had to give up their careers and their normal way of life. And they did it. But that doesn't mean it was easy or an obvious choice for them.

To take it even further, consider the disruption Jesus' resurrection must have brought to the disciples. It was both frightening and joyful. Troubling, yet amazing. It was not as simple as a, "Oh Jesus! We're so happy you've risen from the dead. Of course you told us you would rise on the third day so we were expecting it all along." Because God's breakthroughs always bring new opportunities as well as new challenges, they always require a measure of faith to be recognized and received. We never realize the investment we have in the status quo until it is threatened, even by the answer to our own prayers!

Jesus is patient with us, with our slowness to believe. He understands that we may need a little time.

Luke records in Acts that Jesus met with the disciples over a period of forty days, giving them "many convincing proofs that he was alive." I love the word *many.* It wasn't just one proof or two, but many. That's patience.

Once the breakthrough arrives, it makes sense that we would need faith to embrace it, to believe that God has actually done it.

For me, it took many weeks to believe my dad had actually come to faith. As amazing as the night of his conversion was, every morning I expected my dad to return back to normal. But then, one of my closest friends, Drew, came over to the house to pick me up for a night out, and he had a conversation with my dad in the kitchen. When we got in the car, he asked, "What happened to your dad's face?"

"What do you mean?"

"His face is so different. He looks younger or something. Like the creases and wrinkles have disappeared somehow. He looks more peaceful than I have ever seen him."

If others were seeing the changes, perhaps my dad had really changed. Sometimes it's friends around us who help us recognize the breakthrough when we lack the eyes to see it ourselves. We often need others to help us discern what God is doing.

He must've given his life to Jesus after all.

A new normal. Not only does breakthrough faith enable us to receive God's intervening work, it also establishes a new normal of faith for us. When God breaks through, he doesn't just do it for the benefits of the immediate circumstance at hand, such as my dad's conversion. He also wants to lift us up to a larger level of faith.

Each time Jesus provided a breakthrough, he expected the disciples to walk in the new normal the breakthrough provided. For example, Jesus warned his disciples about the leaven of the Pharisees. They thought he was talking about their lack of bread in the boat, but Jesus rebuked them sternly, "Why are you talking about having no bread? Do you still not see or understand? Are your hearts hardened? Do you have eyes but fail to see, and ears but fail to hear? And don't you remember? When I broke the five loaves for the five thousand, how many basketfuls of pieces did you pick up?"

They had already seen him feed five thousand men and their families, and then more than four thousand others another time. After those experiences, Jesus expected them to be operating at a new level of faith. They shouldn't be focusing on the lack of bread anymore.

In this way, breakthrough faith positions us for something larger—a new normal. Jesus speaks of it: "Whoever can be trusted with very little can also be trusted with much." For me, watching my dad come to faith implanted in me a mustard seed of faith that said, "There is no one Jesus cannot reach." Somewhere in those weeks of watching my dad as a new believer, I made a vow to Jesus, "By your grace, I will never doubt your ability to reach anyone." For me, that was a new level of faith in his saving power.

For Kristina, seeing a breakthrough came while she was sitting in her women's Bible study. A few years had passed since she vowed never to pray for healing again. But after a Chinese American woman told the group that her cancer had progressed to stage four and she only had months to live, the group leader spoke up, "Would you allow us to pray for you?" The tear-filled woman nodded. What happened next stopped Kristina's heart. The group leader turned to look directly at her. "Kristina, would you pray for her to be healed of this cancer?"

She hesitated. The failures of the past still plagued her. Yet, perhaps more from the peer pressure of the moment than a nudge from the Spirit, Kristina placed her hand on the woman's shoulder, and she began to pray, "In Jesus name, cancer, leave this woman's body. You have no place here. Be healed in Jesus' name."

As she prayed, what felt like currents of electricity flowed through her hand into the woman. Hope had reawakened, and with a boldness that surprised Kristina more than anyone, she declared, "In Jesus' name, you are healed."

Weeks passed, however, and the woman had not returned to the Bible study. Kristina's worst fears came back to haunt her: The woman hadn't been healed, and now she's so disappointed she won't come back to the group. But a month later, she did return. She slinked in at the end of a meeting to share how after an examination, her doctor could not find a single trace of the cancer.

In her previous disappointment, Kristina had vowed never to pray for anyone ever again. Since that moment, that vow has been mercifully broken. She regularly prays for others, helping them find healing and wholeness in Jesus' name.

Kristina is operating at a new normal, and new normals are how revivals keep flourishing.

Of course, there are times after reaching one breakthrough that we find ourselves headed back through the U curve, seeking the next breakthrough, navigating the choice between despair and breakthrough yet again. Or perhaps there's something else in our life that needs breakthrough. Sometimes, like the saints in Hebrews 11, we might not see a particular breakthrough in our lifetimes. That doesn't mean something is wrong but actually that something is growing. We still approach faith with hope.

We wouldn't expect God to leave us there at one level of faith. God can always lead us to another, newer normal.

In time, I would see God save my mom. I would pray with some of my brothers as they received Jesus' salvation. I would see my sister, Alysa, get baptized. I would see reconciliation and forgiveness between family members. I would see suicide averted, depression overcome, and unclean spirits sent packing.

God used that mustard seed of faith from my dad's conversion to grow me in an evangelistic calling on college campuses throughout San Diego. In fact, my experience watching God reach my family inspired a ministry philosophy supported by three core convictions: there is no one God can't use; there is no one Jesus can't reach; there is no campus God can't revive. And seeing God move on campus gives me even greater expectancy: there is no church God cannot empower; there is no city that God cannot renew; there is no nation God cannot heal.

Peter and the other disciples experienced the same shift of mind. After his resurrection, Jesus asked them to wait for the Holy Spirit. After ten days, the Holy Spirit was poured out on the men and women gathered in the upper room. And when a crowd of thousands gathered at their doorstep, attracted by the noise and commotion, it was Peter who stood up to cast his nets wide for the catch of a lifetime. Peter had come full circle from that moment on the Sea of Galilee when Jesus first called him to become a fisher of people.

He still had his flaws, but he confronted the Sanhedrin with boldness, healed the lame and sick, raised the dead, helped inaugurate the mission to the Gentiles, and eventually died a martyr's death in Rome being crucified upside-down. As Jesus predicted, Peter's mustard seed–sized faith—imperfect as it was—became the rock upon which a movement was founded.

This new, resurrection faith revived thousands, upended the Roman Empire, and has been transforming the world for the last two millennia.

The Peter in Acts is a new man, operating out of a new normal.

This is breakthrough faith. And revivals are built on breakthroughs, on a season of new normals. This kind of faith, empowered by God's Spirit, inaugurated an age of reviving grace that has changed the world.

Discussion Questions

1. Where on the breakthrough U curve do you find yourself? Why?
2. If you're not already there, what would you need to get to the stage of revived hope?
3. Given where you are on the U curve, what is God saying to you about it? What are the next steps he is asking you to take?

PART TWO
EXPERIENCING REVIVAL

Chapter Four

CONSECRATION

It remains for the world to see what the Lord can do with a man wholly consecrated to Christ.
HENRY VARLEY TO D.L. MOODY

Consecrate yourselves and be holy, because I am the LORD your God. Keep my decrees and follow them. I am the LORD, who makes you holy.
GOD TO ISRAEL, LEVITICUS 20:7-8

It was a typical sunny day in San Diego, usually glorious by any other standard. I (Ryan) sat in a campus coffee shop. It was a modern mix of glass and concrete, and the sidewalks that wrapped around it were dotted by palm trees.

Stephen sat across from me and could barely contain his excitement. With a flash in his eyes, he described the growing intimacy he was having with God. His prayer life was soaring to a new level: "I feel God's presence with me all through the day because I'm constantly asking him and thanking him for his help."

And though I was happy for him, I couldn't push away a disturbing thought: *I haven't felt God in my life like that for a long time.*

As I made the long walk to my car, honest words started to pour out my holy discontent: "God, I am burned out. I've lost touch with you."

On my way to the parking lot, I found myself walking across a freeway overpass and noticed the rushing cars speeding underneath. That was my life. *I'm always in such a hurry, God. I don't even know how to stop anymore. When was the last time I just enjoyed your presence?*

At this point, we've offered a definition of revival and some understanding of its process, but defining revival isn't the same as leading it.

And it's our conviction that we can't lead it unless we've experienced it. We don't have to be experts. Still, it'll be hard to ask other people to jump into the waters of revival without, at least, getting our toes wet.

So when our spiritual batteries are drained, what could we do? To experience revival, consecration is a crucial first step.

The Consecration Equation

To consecrate means to set something apart in dedication for God's special purpose. That's what it means to make it holy. In the Bible, anything and everything can be set apart, from people to animals, physical places, buildings, clothing, a period of time, food, plunder, gold, and silver.

In the beginning, God set apart the seventh day as holy, a day of rest. In Exodus, consecration finds another level, as God asks the Israelites to set apart their firstborn of both children and livestock. Later on Mount Sinai, Moses commanded the Israelites to consecrate themselves. They washed their clothes, abstained from sexual intimacy, and on the third day, waited for God's glory to appear on Mount Sinai. Throughout the book of Leviticus, God's people consecrated everything used in the sacred space of the Tabernacle, from priests to utensils, the altar, and incense.

To take this further, the Bible links consecration with costly sacrifice. God prepared Israel for their first big battle with Jericho by commanding all the men to circumcise themselves—a consecrating act. If you're going into battle, it just doesn't seem like the most pragmatic thing to do!

Jesus himself, before stepping into his ministry, gave up food with a forty-day fast in the desert. Vulnerable among wild animals, Jesus consecrated himself in this way to prepare for his earthly ministry.

But why does God ask for this level of dedication and devotion, giving so much to him when he already owns everything and lacks nothing? Is this just a way to prove ourselves? Is it intended to appease his needs or anger?

Consecration isn't about appeasing the fickle demands of an overbearing deity. It's about making ourselves available to God so he can make us holy, and set us apart for his purposes.

He longs to restore us to the glory of his holiness. It's as if God is saying, "I made you in my image—to be like me. Let me help you come back to who you really are—holy!"

There are two parts to this equation: our part and God's part. Take a look at this verse from Leviticus: "Consecrate yourselves and be holy, because I am the Lord your God. Keep my decrees and follow them. I am the Lord, who makes you holy."

On the one hand, God commands his people to "consecrate yourselves," but he rounds out the verse with "I am the Lord, who makes you holy." In figure 5, we've drawn the line with an arrow at each end to illustrate the tension created by our tendency to emphasize one side of the equation over the other. To fully grasp what it means to consecrate ourselves, we need to understand these two sides.

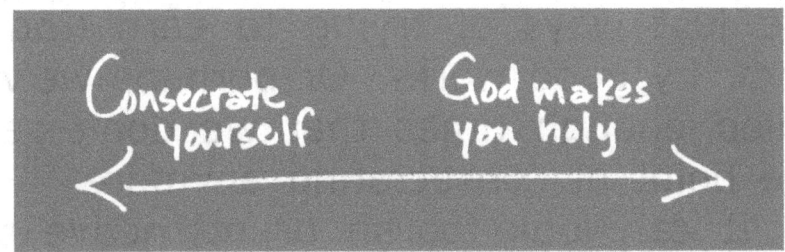

Figure 5. The consecration equation

Our Part: Consecrate Ourselves

In *The Essentials of Prayer*, E.M. Bounds puts it simply, "Consecration is the human side of holiness ... consecration being the intelligent, voluntary act of the believer." Bounds rightly highlights two key insights on our side of the equation.

First, because it's the human side, consecration prevents us from being passive bystanders, keeping us from complacency. Deferring to God doesn't defer our responsibility.

We might have lots of reasons not to consecrate. Some, like me, find consecration too costly. Others just find consecration a bit old-fashioned. Being relevant feels more important than the call to be set apart and different. A few might think that consecrating activities are just ways of trying to earn God's favor by good works. Or perhaps we've failed enough times that we don't see the point of consecrating anymore.

It can look foolish or restrictive to those who don't yet know Jesus, while in the eyes of the hardened religionist, consecration appears naive or worse, fanatical.

But the writer of Hebrews cuts through these objections to remind us of our responsibility: "Make every effort to live in peace with everyone and to be holy; without holiness no one will see the Lord."

Every effort.

Secondly, because consecration is voluntary, it's profoundly and essentially relational. It is a way that we, as human beings, can choose to give ourselves in love to the Lover of our souls. It's not a calculated and carefully measured quid pro quo arrangement, as if we could negotiate or manipulate God into our preferred terms. We can't impress God with it, and we're not supposed to use it to impress others or puff ourselves up.

Instead, when it comes to consecration, picture a wedding. When two people give themselves to each other in marriage, what makes it so special is that both people are choosing to set themselves apart from all other lovers. They are both purposefully limiting themselves from every other option, for the sake of giving themselves completely to one other person.

Theologian Ronald Rolheiser writes:

> Medieval philosophy had a dictum that said: Every choice is a renunciation. Indeed. Every choice is a thousand renunciations. To choose one thing is to turn one's back on many others. To marry one person is to not marry all the others, to have a baby means to give up certain other things; and to pray may mean to miss watching television or visiting with friends. This makes choosing hard. No wonder we struggle so much with commitment.

Choice is the flaming center of true love. And every yes is a thousand noes.

I (Ryan) remember sitting in a coffee shop the week after my honeymoon. I was doing some work, when I noticed that an attractive woman sat next to me. Without even thinking, I quickly hid my hand—with my wedding ring—under the table. It was a reflex:

I was used to presenting myself as available.

But as soon as I realized what I was doing, I pulled my hand out from under the table and raised my hand up high. It was my awkward signal to everyone I was utterly taken—though I'm sure this woman nor anyone else even cared or noticed. It was about my choice to daily set myself apart from all others for my one and only.

God's Part: He Makes Us Holy

On the other side of consecration is God's responsibility. Only God is truly holy, and only God can make us holy. A clear eye on God, who alone makes us holy, guards us from taking pride in our acts of consecration. The truth is, there is always a part of us that loves sin and worldliness.

Before being commissioned to his ministry, Isaiah saw the Lord in a powerful vision. Angels flew around his throne, singing songs of God's glory. Their worship was so strong that it shook doorposts and thresholds. In the presence of such a holy God, Isaiah knew he was done for: "Woe to me! ... I am ruined! For I am a man of unclean lips, and I live among a people of unclean lips." There was nothing he could do.

In response, an angel flew to him with a live coal in his hand and touched it to Isaiah's mouth, yet it didn't sting or sear. The smell of burning flesh was absent. Instead, it was the work of God, where Isaiah's guilt was taken away and his sin atoned. He was consecrated and ready to say, "Here am I. Send me!"

We can't directly change our hearts, but God can. Admitting this is painful, but it's also liberating. If we don't understand this side of the equation, we'll foolishly put our confidence in our efforts alone. That will make us a victim to various spiritual deformities: judgmental of ourselves and others, impatient with mistakes, rigid and legalistic about rules, anxious and fearful of failure. On the outside, we might look good to others, but on the inside we'll become angry, fearful, resentful, and insecure as we try to carry a heavy burden of responsibility that only God can lift.

At other times, we could be blissfully ignorant, out of touch with our own unholiness, dazzled by our own magnificence and achievement. It's in this place that God's mercy triumphs over judgment, and he allows circumstances that are out of our control.

In both of our lives, the difficulty in raising funds for ministry, a prolonged season of searching for a home in an expensive market, or the pain of physical injuries has served to disrupt our daily routines and set us apart for a deeper level of trust in God. Spiritual disciplines are valuable in training for holiness, but often the disciplines we didn't choose are the hardest to accept and therefore have the greatest power to actually transform us.

Only God can do that.

When we put both roles of consecration together—our part and God's part—we find that consecration is something we do that prepares us for what only God can do. It gets us ready to see the wonder of God moving miraculously in the world. Paul wrote it this way: "In a large house there are articles not only of gold and silver, but also of wood and clay; some are for special purposes and some for common use. Those who cleanse themselves from the latter will be instruments for special purposes, made holy, useful to the Master and prepared to do any good work."

In this way, we're like sailors, raising the sail, presenting ourselves to be caught by the wind. The sails don't make the wind come, of course, but they do prepare us to catch it when the moment arrives. At the same time, unlike the wind, God is moved when he sees people preparing themselves for his wonders out of faith, hope, and expectancy.

When Stephen talked about his prayer life, it stirred in me (Ryan) a longing for some sort of breakthrough. Serendipitously, a dear friend offered the use of his guesthouse as a place for study and quiet reflection. Only fifteen minutes away, it was a chance to consecrate myself away from the familiarity of my daily ministry tasks. It was an easy yes.

I walked into the guesthouse with a sense of anticipation, and my eyes landed on a walk-in closet. Immediately, I thought, *This is my prayer closet.* When I shut the door, I also shut out the rest of the world. This closet became my spiritual home almost every day for six months.

As I sat there, I heard God say, "You don't really love being in my presence." It wasn't condemning but instead a severe invirtation. I realized that I could sit in front of my TV for hours, but I couldn't do that with God. And in that realization, a greater hunger grew within me, which built into a full venting of my longing for more of God. It was raw, and uncomfortable. Tears streamed down my face for hours. I prayed, "If I don't get more of you, then something in me will die!" Only God can give us that kind of desire. There is nothing we can do to manufacture a true, passionate love for God's presence.

In that consecrating season, I was being prepared for something more.

The Fruit of Consecration

Consecration reminds us that in our approach to revival, it's not about doing the best we can. Our best just isn't good enough.

Revival can't be about working harder or making slight tweaks in strategy and technique. Otherwise, revival becomes a recipe for burnout rather than a promise of breakthrough. It can't be based on a particular leader's personality, gifts, or ego.

Consecration reminds us that revival is dependent on the Spirit of God. Jesus never asked his disciples to do the best they could; he told them to wait for the Holy Spirit to fill them and empower them.

When we consecrate ourselves, God will fill us with his best to transform our worst. And consecration, done rightly, offers two main fruits: it draws us into deeper *intimacy* with God and produces in us an authentic spiritual *authority*.

It connects us to his presence and his power.

Presence: Intimacy with God

While Moses was on top of the mountain in the fiery presence of God, the people of Israel grew tired of waiting. They plunged themselves into idolatry and created a crisis that threatened to destroy their nation and their relationship with God. As a result, God promised to drive out the inhabitants of the Promised Land before them, but he would no longer go with them. He's basically saying, "You'll get what you've always wanted, but I'm not going with you."

They'd get his power, but not his presence. And to Israel's credit, that wasn't good news. They mourned. They really didn't want the land without their God.

Moses, as their leader, then took a step of consecration. He went outside the camp and into the tent of meeting, where God's presence—symbolized by a pillar of cloud—would fill its entrance. And there (which should blow your mind) God would speak to Moses "face to face, as one speaks to a friend."

A promise without his presence is not enough. Intimacy with God is bedrock, so much so that Moses won't take ahold of the promise without God going with them: "If your Presence does not go with us, do not send us up from here."

In response, God relents: "I will do the very thing you have asked, because I am pleased with you and I know you by name." It's not that God knew what to call him; it's more that he knew Moses through and through, and that intimacy moved God to act.

In another example, the church of Ephesus had done so much good. They had persevered and endured hardship, they had guarded themselves against false doctrines and had rejected the encroaching influence of worldliness. But Jesus had one thing against them: "You have forsaken the love you had at first."

Coming back to our first love is more than getting back to where we've been. It's about loving Jesus more than we've ever loved him before. It's not about large crowds of people, dramatic spiritual experiences, or new ministry strategies. It's about falling more deeply in love with Jesus because love is at the center of revival.

And consecration helps us return to our first love. Henri Nouwen writes, "The question is not: How many people take you seriously? How much are you going to accomplish? Can you show some results? But: Are you in love with Jesus?"

When we consecrate ourselves, we make room for God to rekindle white-hot love for him. The very act of consecration is sacrificial, which itself is in the nature of love. Didn't Jesus say, "Greater love has no one than this: to lay down one's life for one's friends"?

Allowing God to revive this kind of love is the most important thing we can do for ourselves and our leadership. After all, isn't this kind of love reflective of what burns at the center of God's own leadership: "For God so loved the world that he gave his one and only Son"?

God mourns, wrestles, seeks, and sacrifices for us as well with a day-and-night intensity that never ebbs, always flowing out toward us, wooing us into the intimacy of this love. More than anything else, our families need us to be on fire with God; our coworkers and friends need us wrapped in God's glory afresh; our world, above all else, needs us overflowing with the heat of God's fiery love.

Nouwen underlines this necessity: "The central question is, are the leaders of the future truly men and women of God, people with an ardent desire to dwell in God's presence, to listen to God's voice, to look at God's beauty, to touch God's incarnate Word and to taste fully God's infinite goodness?"

I (James) was speaking at a student conference, nestled in a wooded portion of the Shenandoah Valley. It was a consecrated time, set apart to be with God. After teaching about how to hear God's voice, I led a listening prayer experience. I basically asked the students to picture themselves coming face to face with Jesus and to listen to what he had to say. The house lights were up, and no background music set any mood.

Afterward an engineering student came up to me to tell his story. He had considered himself a Christian all his life, but during that time of prayer, he heard God say this phrase to him—not necessarily as an audible voice but in an outside thought that came into his mind—"You are my son." And with tears welling up in his eyes and a slight tremble in his voice, I could tell that nothing else mattered. Six years later, he serves as a campus minister, helping students know the love he experienced that evening. That's what love does.

Power: Authentic Spiritual Authority

On Mount Tabor, Jesus, along with James, John, and Peter, soaked deeply in God's presence, so much so that the biblical text echoes Moses' time in the tent of meeting. For Moses, his face shone so brilliantly he had to wear a veil. For Jesus, his clothes became dazzlingly bright, "whiter than anyone in the world could bleach them."

But when they come down from the mountain, the contrast couldn't be greater between his direct authority and the disciples' empty gestures and entangled arguments.

The disciples had cast out demons before. Why couldn't they now? He did not tell them they got the formula wrong, or that they had failed to name the demon correctly, or that they hadn't recognized the inner healing that needed to happen, or that they hadn't shouted loud enough.

He said nothing about technique or strategy. Instead he tells them, "This kind can come out only by prayer." Jesus directed them to the very thing he had just been doing—consecrating himself. We'll miss the point if we see prayer as another strategy. Jesus wasn't saying that they hadn't prayed enough or rightly. Jesus is telling them something altogether different: to use God's power, you need to be in God's presence.

For example, a visiting team of InterVarsity campus ministers from New England had come out to San Diego to learn from our strategies and models of ministry. When I (Ryan) asked Jesus how I should lead our meetings, I sensed I should focus on how he had taught us to pray and seek his face. One of those campus ministers, Sarah Cowan Johnson, wrote up a reflection of her visit:

> I appreciate that, over the course of three days with us, Ryan resisted the temptation to describe UCSD's strategies, or even tell many stories of the kind of growth and conversion they have seen over the last decade. His conviction here came from his experience with previous visitors, past pilgrimages like ours, where folks came to see something unprecedented and miraculous, came away with a few key strategies to reproduce, but missed the critical significance of the UCSD team seeking the Lord persistently over weeks and weeks ahead of employing these strategies. So these folks would return home, try to reproduce UCSD's strategies without seeking the Lord in their own context and, not surprisingly, would see little fruit.

The thought that came to my mind as Ryan described this phenomenon was that these replicated strategies were like "copies of copies"—the more times you photocopy an original, the quality and potency decreases.

Strategy without spiritual authority and power is anemic.

Of course, we can always learn from others, but here's the catch. We must consecrate the offering of our strategies and best practices so that, out of a deeper intimacy with God, fresh spiritual authority and power can animate otherwise lifeless conduits of our programs. Pastor Jordan Seng connects consecration and power this way: "By connecting self-sacrifice and power, God helps ensure that the most powerful ministers will also be the most able to love selflessly."

Spiritual authority isn't about technique, skill, or even effort. It's about the overflow of having met with God in intimacy.

Jesus sustained an authentic spiritual authority that never dissipated into worn-out formulas or gimmicks. And from that authority, he was thoroughly creative and original. Jesus engaged each person differently: a finger in one person's ear, a saliva-mud salve on blind eyes for another, a word of healing to one, a healing touch for another.

Without this kind of intimacy and authority, we will slip into a pantomime of personalities and methods, just photocopies of decreasing quality. That is not what God has created us to lead from.

Instead, God has created every one of us to lead from his storehouse of immeasurable power. And this power is necessary because we face greater powers that seek to oppose us. Lloyd-Jones writes, "You must realize that you are confronted by something that is too deep for your methods to get rid of, or to deal with, and you need something that can go down beneath that evil power, and shatter it, and there is only one thing that can do that, and that is the power of God."

When leading revival, we don't need less of God's power to glide with the tide. We actually need more to do the things God is calling us to do because revival is impossible without his grace and help.

D.L. Moody, a nineteenth-century revivalist, had the largest Sabbath school and congregation in Chicago. He was satisfied and didn't feel the need for more of God's power and authority. But in 1871, two elderly women challenged him to his face, "You need power." He initially rebuffed it, saying that they should pray for someone else, but they insisted.

But after a few weeks, something stirred in him. A great hunger entered his soul, desiring for more power for service. He kept asking God to fill him with his Spirit. For the next four months, he dedicated himself to prayer toward this filling. On October 8, 1871, a terrible fire swept through Chicago and burned Moody's church to the ground. He didn't have the money to rebuild the church. Feeling helpless, he took a trip to New York City to, as he put it, "beg" for money.

While walking up Wall Street, between the towering financial buildings and the hustle and bustle of the crowd,

Moody was overcome with the answer to his prayers for God's power. Here's how he describes it:

> Well, one day, in the city of New York—O—what a day! I cannot describe it; I seldom refer to it; it is almost too sacred an experience to me. Paul had an experience of which he never spoke for fourteen years. I can only say, God revealed Himself to me, and I had such an experience of His love that I had to ask Him to stay His hand. I went on preaching again. The sermons were not different; I did not present any new truths, and yet hundreds were converted. I would not be placed back where I was before that blessed experience if you would give me all of Glasgow.

From that season of consecration, Moody's ministry exploded and took on an international level of influence that exceeded anything he could have imagined. It wasn't an impartation of new strategy but rather an endowment of power.

In the kingdom of God, intimacy precedes power. It's not to be mistaken for emotionalism or sensation seeking. It's about returning to our first love.

Consecration for the Rest of Us

When God stirs our hearts with hunger and longing, we respond by consecrating ourselves. Revival leaders set themselves apart for more.

What's your next step?

Start with confession. Many revivals start with confession, whether private or public. It's costly to face the truth. Still, Isaiah's response in the presence of a holy God is a right and justified response, since it reminds us of the truth of who we are. None of us are holy on our own. All of us are in need of mercy and rescue.

The Pyongyang Revival, considered the birthplace of Korean Protestantism, found a groundswell at a ten-day Bible conference in January 1907. The evenings were open to the public, so about fifteen hundred had gathered. On the first night, missionary William Blair preached out of 1 Corinthians 12 to show that "hate in a brother's heart brought pain to Christ, the church's Head." That night, some confessed a lack of love for others, particularly for the Japanese who oppressed them, and one church officer confessed his hidden hatred for another.

The next night, the missionaries leading the conference felt spiritually blocked. They felt no life in the meeting, which pressed them to pray more earnestly before the next nightly gathering. When they entered the third night, the spiritual atmosphere felt different, that the "room was full of God's presence."

That night, Graham Lee, a conference organizer, asked the people to pray out loud, all together. As the night went on, people began to weep and confess their sins. Missionary William Blair recounts Lee's retelling of the night:

> Man after man would rise, confess his sins, break down and weep, and then throw himself to the floor and beat the floor with his fists in perfect agony of conviction.... Again, after another confession, they would break out in

uncontrollable weeping, and we would all weep, we could not help it. And so the meeting went on until two o'clock a.m., with confession and weeping and praying.

It went even bigger on the night after, as missionaries confessed their hatred of each other and asked for forgiveness. So much so that Blair would write, "Every sin a human being can commit was publicly confessed that night.... We may have our theories of the desirability or undesirability of public confession of sin. I have had mine; but I know now that when the Spirit of God falls upon guilty souls, there will be confession, and no power on earth can stop it." From this time, Korean Protestantism was born and grew, so much so that today South Korea has the largest churches in the world and is, per capita, the largest missionary-sending country in the world.

So where do we start today? Our first suggestion is to find a confessor. In some Christian traditions, that might be a priest or minister. But if that person isn't available, look for someone who exhibits a mature faith, is someone you trust, and who can keep confidences. Be open and honest, and freedom will come.

I (James) have three young kids, while my wife also cares for her ailing parents. We both work, so our lives are quite full. But still I'll peel away near bedtime once a month to connect with a dear friend over a video call. We'll take time to walk through seven spiritual questions and pray for each other. It's always tough to answer the second question: What do you need to confess since our last meeting?

So much in my pride wants to hide, manage, spin, and soften my sins, but when I fully confess, I find that I have more strength to walk in holiness.

I've heard it said, "We're only as sick as our secrets."

As the Spirit moves, you also may have opportunity to confess more publicly, whether in a small group or a larger setting. And perhaps that could, in turn, create a space for others to freely confess their sins. This cannot be forced; to do so would only make it feel fake or manipulative. But as the Spirit convicts of sin, it might be good to allow it to continue so that more people can consecrate themselves and let God make them holy.

Do something costly. Ask Jesus to lead you to give up something sacrificially. It could be almost anything: food, social media, alcohol, caffeine, your phone, sleep, or video games. It just has to be costly. Be like David who said, "I will not sacrifice to the Lord my God burnt offerings that cost me nothing."

When I (Ryan) was about to turn forty, I needed fresh fire for revival. Tina, a friend of mine, texted me, pointing out that the next day would mark the beginning of a forty-day period leading up to my birthday. And she sensed God inviting me to fast for that entire time. Easy for her to say!

I didn't want to admit it, but I knew God was in it.

Those forty days were challenging and difficult, yet glorious. My stomach's ache for food merged with my soul's ache for an outpouring of the Spirit. Whenever the hunger pangs struck, I would pray, "Father, my stomach hungers for food, but my soul hungers for you even more!" Once it was over, I actually missed the raw physical longing I felt for God. As a result, my faith and passion for revival went far deeper into my soul. I credit the intensity of my fervor today to those hunger-filled days.

Instead of forty days, you could go ten. Or three. But do something you feel the Lord leading you to do. And since almost anything can be consecrated, feel free to be more creative.

While in college, I (James) had been praying for the gift of prophecy for six months. I was following the biblical command: to eagerly seek the greater gifts. In this season, I was studying at my desk when a fellow fraternity brother, Miles, walked into my room. He stood six feet four, and add four more inches because of the way he wore his hair. But his constantly sleepy look from behind his glasses and his dry sense of humor could put anyone at ease.

Right on my desk was a thirty-disc CD collection full of my R & B favorites from the eighties and nineties. If you don't know groups like Guy, Troop, and Bell Biv Devoe, then you just don't know music! He started reading the song titles out of one of them, and I was particularly struck by the overt sensuality of the lyrics.

At that moment, I knew that God was asking me to throw them out. It was a way to clean house, to set my life apart. And it was costly; I loved my music, and they weren't cheap! What a waste! But when I did, I immediately received the gift of prophecy. I had to cleanse my listening to really hear from God.

A friend of mine, Jordan Seng, has a great example from his own life. When he was in graduate school, he also traveled often to do prophetic ministry. But he felt that his "worldly senses and considerations were compromising my spiritual ministry of prophecy and prayer." He wanted to get better control over what he focused on in life.

So he blindfolded himself for a better part of a week in what he called a "sight fast." It couldn't have been easy, bumping into furniture, eating, and just getting through a day. Then make it a week! Still, he said that "the sight fast quieted my senses so that I could interact with people and situations with a more pronounced spiritual sight."

Not only has he continued to do something like a sight fast from time to time, he also has, as a pastor, prescribed this kind of fast for "people (mostly men) whose visual appetites were drifting out of control in one way or another." His reasoning? "Every sense has an appetite associated with it, and it can be enormously helpful to lay a sense aside forcefully from time to time."

Inspired by this story, I have also set aside other consecration periods. I had a time in my life when I was watching a lot of movies and television shows. For Lent I gave up these Hollywood stories so I could tell a better story about Jesus. After that period, I did feel that my evangelistic gifts were far more Spirit-empowered. For another Lent, when I felt like I was finding myself envious of other people's successes, I gave up social media. This may speak of the addictive nature of social media, but out of the fasts I've done, I found this one to be the hardest. Without digital distractions, I found myself at the mercy of my darker thoughts, and I had to invite God into those thoughts through prayer rather than try to act as if they didn't exist.

None of these consecration activities are meant to comfort us. Instead, they press into our dissatisfaction. But God uses activities like these to create deeper intimacy and connection within each of us.

They set us apart.

Discussion Questions

1. For you, personally, what is your part in consecration? What is God's part?
2. In the past, how has consecration affected your intimacy and authority in God?
3. What costly, consecrating activity do you sense the Spirit leading you into now?

Chapter Five

CALLING

Every response to a call necessitates a leap of faith.
GREGG LEVOY, *CALLINGS*

Lord, if it's you, ... tell me to come to you on the water.
PETER, TO JESUS, MATTHEW 14:28

Four hundred students were about to cram into UCSD's Price Center Theater. It was our largest outreach of the spring quarter, and I (Ryan) felt a holy prompting to do something different. I wanted to make a public invitation to faith.

We hadn't done this before. No one had seen anything like that in our ministry either. So when I mentioned this, the anxiety level of the outreach team shot up like a rocket. They said stuff like: What if no one responds? What if it makes everyone feel awkward and our friends never want to come back? There's no way they'll make a decision to follow Jesus in front of others.

They even started to say that UCSD students were different. The university was dominated by biology and engineering majors, so the students, they said, were more intellectual. They obviously wouldn't respond to something that seemed so emotional.

To be honest, I felt the same concerns.

But I also felt called.

A Call to Revival

Calling, in general, is fundamental to the way God relates to us.

The Bible is a calling-studded story from Genesis to Revelation, with a far-flung cast of characters who hear the call of God and respond. Abraham was called to leave his household and go to a new land. Moses was called to go back to Egypt to face Pharaoh, Esther was called to intervene for her people, and Mary, as a virgin, was called to bear the child that would save the world. And so on.

But with revivals, calling takes on an even greater importance because vision isn't enough. Revival leaders need calling.

A call to revival starts us on the breakthrough U curve in the first place, nourishing a holy discontent. It's a provocateur against comfort, prodding us toward an alternate vision of what God can do—into a season of breakthrough, into a new normal. We might be called to do something that is unprecedented in our life, something we never thought we would or could ever do. We might be led into something impossible, something far bigger than we'd be able to do on our own.

But not only does a call breathe faith into our holy dissatisfaction, it can also foster the determination to do it. Vision shows you what's possible; calling compels you to do something about it. A vision tells you that the kingdom of God can break through; calling shows you how God is asking you to be a part of it.

"The point is this," confirms author Reggie McNeal. "It is tough enough to serve as a Christian with a call. Without it, the choice constitutes cruel and unusual self-punishment."

I (Ryan) feel almost sheepish sharing this, because it hasn't yet come to pass. But almost a decade ago, I had returned from sabbatical. While preparing for a sermon, I became acutely aware of God's presence. I immediately fell to my knees and opened my Bible, and as I prayed, I saw a mental picture of giant double doors hanging in the sky. When Jesus lifted me up to them, I saw more and more doors, scattered throughout San Diego County. I asked Jesus what these doors were about, and he simply said, "You already know."

Then, I did know. Opening these doors would mean a breakthrough of God's Spirit in San Diego. They were doors to revival. I saw myself as a small child trying to pry open these massive doors. I pulled and tugged. But no matter how hard I tried, I couldn't make them budge.

Then Jesus walked toward me holding a golden key, bigger than my torso, and he handed it to me. I asked him what the key was about, and he said, "It is my Spirit." After that, he gave me a Bible reference that was unfamiliar to me. When I looked up Zechariah 4:6, it said: "'Not by might nor by power, but by my Spirit,' says the Lord Almighty." Jesus continued to speak, promising that he would teach me how to have intimacy with his Spirit and how to seek him and lead others toward revival.

Ninety minutes passed before I got up from the floor. My soul was a bonfire. And I also knew what I had to do next: I felt called to stop pursuing a church pastoral position and instead to accept a new position with InterVarsity, serving all of the campuses throughout San Diego County.

But when I first started talking about revival to my new team, I failed to lead a helpful process. I now realize that I alienated people unnecessarily. Without the full support of my team, I considered quitting my position, feeling alone, exhausted, and afraid that I was more of a burden than a blessing.

In it all, my call to revival kept me from running away.

Our dreams can falter in the short term, but a calling can sustain us. When we plunge into a crisis of faith, a call can help us find something solid to grasp. Whether it's a persistent cancer that hasn't responded to our prayers, a cloud of apathy that won't lift from our congregations, or the stubborn unbelief of someone we've been praying would come to faith, a calling can help us remember where true north lies.

A call helps us cling to God with extraordinary humility and desperation. And if obeyed, a call brings us into equally extraordinary intimacy with our Father.

Often, a call to revival can lead us into confrontation with powers and principalities. It will be clear that they are well beyond our feeble strength. These kinds of callings put us in direct opposition to overwhelming forces of evil in the world, although we know we stand in Jesus' greater authority. And when faced with these evil challenges, a calling grounds us.

Then how do we receive this kind of calling? Peter's life can offer three steps to help us receive our own calling to follow.

Step One: Recognize What Jesus Is Doing

The storm came with little warning, even to seasoned fishermen. Fatigue ached with every pull of the oars as Peter and the rest of the disciples worked against the wind and waves that now buffeted their little boat. It had already been a long day, administering food to five thousand families. But the joy and wonder of that moment had long dissipated as the disciples labored against tireless headwinds.

After many hours and against all effort, they found themselves helplessly adrift somewhere in the middle of a raging sea. The stinging cold water whipped their faces. The enveloping darkness shut out all sense of direction.

The storm was bigger than they were, and they were scared.

Just before dawn, the disciples see something even scarier than their storm. A ghost was walking on the water toward them. What was bad, just got worse.

But it's not a ghost, it's Jesus. And upon recognizing him, Peter knew what he would do next.

Before this moment, it would be safe to guess that Peter would never have come up with the idea of walking on water. He's a fisherman. He gets it. Stormy waters usually got people sunk. But as he sat there, gawking in disbelief, something stirred in Peter. He put two and two together and saw that since his rabbi was doing it, he should do it as well.

After all, that's what disciples do: they do the things the rabbi did for the reasons he did them.

It's an age-old pattern. Jesus did the same: he would only do what he saw his Father doing. "Very truly I tell you, the Son can do nothing by himself; he can do only what he sees his Father doing, because whatever the Father does the Son also does."

This is what's happening when Peter sees Jesus.

We are called to follow this same pattern. The Father loves us and is eager to show us where and how he is calling us to be revived and bring revival. In fact, I believe he is showing us all the time, but we'll need to learn how to recognize him. Author Gregg Levoy shares the same sentiment: "We need to learn to recognize our calls in many disguises."

This leads us to the question, How do we learn to see what Jesus is doing in a way that will give rise to our calling? Here are two specific pathways: recognizing what Jesus did in Scripture and what he did in history. (In chapter 10 we'll also talk about discerning what God is doing through community.)

Recognize what Jesus did in Scripture. Above all, the Bible is the most important place we find Jesus awakening our calling. The Scriptures open a doorway to a story that's rich with incredible examples of men and women hearing God's call and choosing to obey. These stories are meant to animate our imagination so that we begin to have visions and dreams of where Jesus is calling us to seek revival.

In my (Ryan's) life, I was reading the story of Jesus' healing and preaching ministry in the towns from Mark's Gospel. I stepped back from my desk, Bible in hand, and sat on the ground. I spent time visualizing the whole scene and then put myself in the picture. I imagined the warmth of the sun on my shoulders, the feel of the crowd pressing in all around us, even the kicked-up dust in my eyes. I saw myself just behind Jesus' right shoulder.

As this scene unfolded, I suddenly saw Jesus turn to me and smile. He wanted to show me something. At this point it felt as though the mental picture had taken on a life of its own. Jesus bent down and prayed for a crippled woman. Her face went from a twisted contortion of pain to wide-eyed wonder. In this image, she pulled herself up and stood erect for the first time in countless years. The sight of the joy and awe in her eyes still brings me to tears.

Then Jesus turned to me and said, "It's that simple, Ryan. You don't have to do anything. Just trust me and let me do the work."

Fast-forward a week: I had just finished having breakfast and catching up with my good friend Erik. As we made our way out of the crowded diner, Erik stopped to talk to a friend we'll call Bill, and I noticed he was walking with a limp. When asked about it, Bill replied, "Actually, to be honest, my foot is in a lot of pain right now. Nothing seems to make the pain go away."

Then he paused, leaving an awkward silence. Right there, the image of Jesus' words come back to me: "Just trust me and let me do the work." I sensed God wanted me to pray for him but I froze.

The moment passed, and we wrapped up the conversation and left the diner. But I couldn't escape Jesus' words. I knew he was calling me to take a risk and pray for this guy. So, although I had never done anything like this before, I went back in.

Finding Bill seated alone at a booth, I walked up to him and asked, "I know this might sound kind of weird, but when you shared about your foot hurting, I felt like Jesus wanted me to come back and pray for your foot to be healed. Are you okay with that?"

"Sure! Why not?" he said, and he immediately stuck his foot out from under the table.

I bent over and gently cradled his foot in my hand. A part of me asked myself, *What in the world are you doing right now?* But it was too late to back out. I prayed in Jesus' name for his foot to be healed and gently placed his foot back on the ground. He stood up, and he felt no pain. When Erik called me a week later, he confirmed that Bill's pain had left for good.

For me, this was an entirely new mode of expressing Jesus' love to others. But seeing Jesus heal in Scripture had made me receptive to his calling in a way I never would have imagined on my own.

Scripture can activate our imaginations when we put ourselves into the account. We can journal a list of Jesus' works and ask the Spirit to highlight the ones that he wants to lead us into further. We could pay attention to our own curiosity, excitement, and even fearful reactions to the idea of doing what we see Jesus doing.

When we read this way, the Scriptures become a road map into the kingdom life we were meant to live. Scripture is more than a devotional tool, it is the prodding stick toward a radical Jesus lifestyle that presses into revival.

Recognize what Jesus did in history. Many people seeking revival have drawn on men and women who came before for inspiration to lead them out of the confines of their limited experience and thinking. Martin Luther took inspiration from the writings of Augustine to help him break out of the Roman Catholic Church's medieval theology. Reading the work of someone who had come earlier opened Luther's eyes to see truths in Scripture he had never seen before.

What if we read from traditions not of our own and tried to recognize Jesus in other streams of Christian faith? We often filter Jesus through our own particular streams of Christianity, so we might need help to widen our lenses. We can be swift to cast judgment or write people off too quickly. What if we were more curious and open? We don't have to agree with everything from someone else's life to find inspiration in it.

Let's chew the meat and spit out the bones, meaning we can read with both openness and biblical discernment. For example, Martin Luther's life and writings are a tremendous inspiration for me and for many evangelicals. His writings on justification by faith are meats I chew and swallow wholeheartedly. But his racist views on Jewish people, expressed in his later years, I spit out.

I (Ryan) remember sitting spellbound as I read about Welsh pastor Evan Roberts's earnest seeking after God in prayer and energetic preaching campaigns around Wales in *The Welsh Revival of 1904* by Eifion Evans. The book recounted story after story of the most spiritually hardened people coming to faith. Coal miners prayed together in the mines for salvation of their loved ones. Family members reconciled their feuds in Jesus' name. To me, it was a report of heaven touching earth, with people talking about the revival in the store, on their commutes, at work, in homes, and anywhere people ran into each other.

It steeled my conviction that when God is on the move, there isn't anyone God can't reach, any sin God cannot break through, and any place God won't revive. Like Peter seeing Jesus walking on water, I remember thinking, *Jesus can do that? How can I be a part of that?* It has inspired me into revival leadership ever since.

Generally, if we haven't experienced something, it'll be hard for us to believe it and doubly hard to put it into practice. Opening ourselves up to hear the wisdom and the stories of those outside our particular stream of Christianity will help us experience—even if by proxy—aspects of Jesus' life that we might never find in our home church or campus fellowship.

Instead of looking down on people from another Christian faith tribe, what if we opened up ourselves to learn from them?

Let's not allow contempt to keep us from wonder.

We don't have to leave our communities, but we'll need examples from outside our camps to strengthen our ability to recognize Jesus' calling on our lives.

Step Two: Ask Before You Walk

Water walking, even on the best of days, is an impossible feat. There is no precedent for Peter to look back to. Moses never did it; neither did David nor any of the prophets. Some came close, as they parted rivers and seas, but no one had ever walked on water.

Yet, in the fear, something in Peter was stirred to life when he saw Jesus. He could've just begged Jesus to quickly get in their boat, or had him calm the storm, but Peter had pluck; he wanted to walk with Jesus instead. The other disciples must've thought him crazy.

So, he asked Jesus to call him out on the water. It's an audacious ask.

Audacity has two sides to it with words like *bold* and *risk taker* on one side, but with other words like *presumptuousness, nerve,* and *impudence* on the other.

In short, audacity is both inspiring and offensive.

It's a faith-filled audacity that caused Francis of Assisi to strip himself naked and pursue a life of poverty in order to revive the simplicity and purity of a corrupted church. Evan Roberts boldly asked God for a revival that would bring in over one hundred thousand converts.

Heidi Baker's story. Heidi Baker audaciously embraced her calling to preach, even though she'd never seen a woman do it. Eventually she'd fulfill a call to go to Mozambique. She asked God for the poorest of the poor, the disregarded, abandoned, unwanted, disease-ridden children of the nation. As she took each step, one at a time, in obedience to her calling, it grew to include a vision to care for one million children.

Her calling has earned her derision, anger, a bounty on her head, threats to her life and family, hunger, and sleepless nights. At the same time, above it all, she experienced unimaginable miracles and some of the most inspiring encounters with Jesus I have ever read.

In one particular story, Heidi and her team of children visited a village that was resistant to the gospel. In fact, the villagers threw rocks at them as they prayed for a blind man to be healed. But after his sight was restored, the villagers dropped their stones and stood in wonder. The now-seeing man immediately began shouting his testimony of healing and about his new faith in Jesus. Through this miracle, a revival swept through the village, with many people receiving Jesus as their Lord and Savior.

In short, Heidi Baker learned to walk on water.

The audacity of a call to revival means we will face pushback, resistance, misunderstandings, and at times even hostility from others. Sometimes that's the cost and sacrifice of asking for what God stirs in us.

But despite the challenges, this kingdom audacity can't be impulsive, reactive, or forceful. When our audacity is grounded in faith, it is tempered by the humility of waiting to ask God—and the patience to listen for the answer.

That's why getting the asking part is so important, because we can't make it happen. Only God can.

So don't be afraid to ask for big things. God is "able to do immeasurably more than all we ask or imagine." But remember, it is asking. It assumes the humility and patience to wait for the confirmation. This will guard us against hubris and strengthen us when the challenges come.

We need to ask before we jump.

How do we ask today? First, listen for God's voice in prayer. God will continue to confirm and speak to us as we ask for direction. God promises, "I will instruct you and teach you in the way you should go; I will counsel you with my loving eye on you."

Second, seek wise counsel. Proverbs says, "The way of fools seems right to them, but the wise listen to advice." We seek God's voice through trusted counsel. Look for friends or mentors who have some maturity or experience in the direction of the calling you're discerning.

Third, obey what God has already given you to do. Waiting and seeking God is not passive. Obeying what Jesus has already given us to do will put us in a posture where we're more likely to discern and receive what God has in store.

Fourth, what we hear may change. Even if we heard something rock-solid in the past, God can give us a new leading, something that could even seem to contradict what we've heard before. In Genesis 22:2, Abraham clearly heard God tell him to sacrifice his son. Ten short verses later, Abraham clearly heard God tell him to stay his hand. If Abraham sacrifices his son at that point, he's disobeying God, even though he clearly heard him say the opposite earlier.

Dallas Willard sums this up nicely: "We must therefore make it our primary goal not just to hear the voice of God, but to be mature people in a loving relationship with him. Only in this way will we hear him rightly."

Finally, realize that our calling might not come all at once. The call for Peter, in this passage, happens in a flash. But it often doesn't come so quickly in our lives. More often than not, it may take time for God to confirm our calling.

It's not because God is hard of hearing, but we actually may need more time to believe. God could be preparing us for what he has to say. Sometimes we're simply not ready to receive our calling: remember Jonah, a prophet who would rather run to the farthest end of the earth than obey what God asked him to do? Rather than in a moment, our calling may be revealed piecemeal—in little bits at a time so we can digest the bigger picture.

It could also come like a big jigsaw puzzle. If we keep track of each piece that God is giving us along the way, we could look back over the words God has spoken to us through Scripture, people, and circumstances. As we meditate on what God has already said, we could begin to see if the pieces connect to some larger picture.

Step Three: Get Out of Your Boat

Out on the water, Jesus beckons Peter to come. Now Peter has a choice. He's heard the call. He can stay in the relative comfort of the boat—at least, he knows what that's about. Or he can get out of the boat and step onto the water toward Jesus. He heard his call. Will he obey or ignore it?

Once we have received confirmation of our calling, we need to obey it. A call to revival puts us at the edge of a proverbial cliff. With the yawning distance between us and the waters below, our hearts race with second thoughts and nagging doubts. When the time has come to jump, we need to do it immediately. If we stand too long on the edge, we risk losing our nerve.

Still, even if we obey, the calling always comes with risks and rewards.

Risks of obeying your call. Peter walked on water. He actually did. But we have no idea how far he got before he got distracted by the wind and rain. He also sank.

For many people seeking revival, obeying their calling meant risking failure, hardship, and loss of comfort, reputation, safety, and even their lives. I think there is a corollary between how high the calling is and the potential dangers they risk.

Some years ago, I (James) was asked to teach about the Holy Spirit at a student conference. And when it's taught, it needs to be demonstrated.

So after a teaching in the morning, I wanted to give an example of listening to God for others. The plan: pick someone out of the crowd and offer prophetic words to that person in front of everyone. The butterflies were swarming in my stomach.

I felt led to pick a young man in a red flannel shirt. His arms were crossed defensively, and he wore his white baseball cap so low that it covered his eyes. His body language was obviously the "I'm-not-going-to-receive-anything-you-have-to-say" vibe, but I went for it anyway.

As NFL coach Bruce Arians says, "No risk it, no biscuit." Right?

I asked him to stand, and he reluctantly did. Then I started to share what I thought God was telling me about him. With each word, the crowd of almost two hundred students "hmm'd" in approval.

But when I asked that student if the words connected, he just kept his arms crossed and immediately said, "Nope." I gave it a few more shots, and each time it seemed that his friends were nodding in agreement. Yet he continued to shoot down every word without a second thought.

My face flushed red, and I could feel sweat beading at my brow. This wasn't going well.

Later, I found out that he and a small group of conservative Christians didn't believe in supernatural gifts and had come already closed to the idea of the weekend's teachings. So he was dug in; he wasn't going to be open to anything.

But still, it made for an awkward start, and I didn't know what God would do with the mess.

With every leap there is always the risk of flopping. And I tell the story to share one that didn't go well. It's a good lesson to learn, although not a fun one: I could fail in front of others, and I'm still alive. Breath still flows through my lungs. And God could—and eventually would—still move powerfully throughout the rest of the weekend.

You need to embrace risk to receive your call. Risk isn't a bad thing. It's actually what gives your faith a fighting chance to grow.

John Wimber often said, "Faith is spelled: R-I-S-K."

By taking these God-appointed risks in our lives, we learn Jesus' trustworthiness firsthand. New normals of confidence in God's faithfulness will lead us ever upward into the heights of faith, positioning us for greater assignments.

And like Peter, sometimes we'll fail. In fact, if you're young and you're not failing at something, I wonder if you're risking enough.

No one, except Jesus, has ever obeyed their calling perfectly. So it's sad that some people feel so comfortable casting self-righteous judgments on the mistakes and imperfections of past revival leaders.

No doubt we can point fingers at Peter's denial of Jesus, David's sins against Uriah, or even the stubborn, rough edges of Paul's personality. In history, Aimee Semple McPherson, who healed thousands of people as documented by the American Medical Association, couldn't heal her own marriages. John Wesley had failures in his Georgia mission, including crossing emotional intimacy boundaries with married women. It's what led him, heart heavy, to Aldersgate.

Yet God used them all. The higher the calling, the more public our imperfections can become. That's the risk. Maybe a reason for our callings is to expose our imperfections, so Jesus can transform us in the process.

Don't be surprised by that sinking feeling. Instead, see it as a natural part of the journey. Jesus won't let us drown. But when those moments come, remember what Peter did. He called out to Jesus, and Jesus was there to lift him up when his faith faltered.

Notice what Jesus didn't say. He didn't say, "Well, Peter, you've made your bed, now lie in it." Or, "I hope you learned your lesson, Peter. Water walking is for deities only." Instead, Jesus caught him and then asked him questions to help him understand what was happening.

We'll be tempted to doubt our calling somewhere along the way. Rest assured, Jesus will be there to lift us up, if we call on him. Our calling can help us out of the crisis of faith at the bottom of the U curve, because we know he's the one who got us out on the water in the first place.

Being called means we can say to Jesus, "You got me into this, and you are the one who will get me through this."

It means that we're never alone.

Rewards of obeying your call. At the same time, the reward for obeying our calling far outweighs the risks. Callings are first and foremost summons to deeper intimacy with Jesus. God's presence will go with us where he is calling us. We will gain a greater awareness of his presence, and so will those around us. Knowing this promise is the absolute key to overcoming the many fears, doubts, and dangers of getting out of our boats. Heidi Baker has learned to lean into this promise and she counsels us accordingly:

> Ask Him to transform you in His love. Worship Him and wait upon Him until you are overwhelmed to the point of no return. If you drink daily from the river of God and stay immersed in Him, then with increasing measure you will begin to pour out a love that is irresistible. As you minister to the broken, the dying, and the hurting, God's holy presence will overflow and spill forth.

We're not called to burn out; we're called to overflow. Overflow is our reward for obeying our calling. When we overflow, we get to watch the Spirit spill forth to others.

Peter actually walked on water. It's historic. No one other than Jesus had done this before. And his water walking had an impact on the rest of the disciples. After Jesus and Peter returned to the boat, the Bible records, "Then those who were in the boat worshiped him, saying, 'Truly you are the Son of God.'"

Peter's obedience results in true worship. When we obey Jesus' calling, we glorify God in a way that causes others to recognize him for who he truly is and worship. This is the story of revivals. Men and women become water walkers, and the resulting onlookers worship Jesus.

Our callings transform us, to be sure, but they are also meant to awaken others with a vision of Jesus that inspires their callings as well. That's the domino effect and the contagious nature of revivals. There is great joy when we walk on water. There is an even greater reward to inspiring others to take their leap of faith.

After prayer and deliberation, our outreach team realized that we were captive to our fears. We were afraid that no one would respond. For some, that might seem silly, but it almost derailed the call God was putting on our ministry. We didn't have to convert anyone. That's God's responsibility. We just had to give people an opportunity.

The time had come. Looking up from my notes, I (Ryan) paused as I surveyed the crowd. Then, I invited people to follow Jesus. I asked them to stand up in front of others and walk to the front.

I waited.

To the leadership team's great joy and relief, twelve people not only stood that night but also made their way to the front of the room. I led them in a prayer of faith to accept Jesus as Lord and Savior. We followed up with them and helped them join our community.

This event had an unexpected ripple effect.

Students started telling me they had friends who might be ready to respond to a public invitation to follow Jesus, but they didn't want to wait for the next outreach. What a change! With encouragement from the team, we started giving calls to faith during our weekly gatherings.

We persevered for six months, seeing little fruit. One student who decided to follow Jesus during this time fell away from faith in a short month. Doubts started to pound down the door of my mind. *Maybe these public invitations are a waste of time. Just give up!*

Fast forward to the next semester. It's the second week of school, and I coached one of our campus ministers to give the call to faith at our second gathering of the year. It was a risky move because it would set the tone with all the incoming freshmen.

My ministry colleague Sarah gave the call at the end of her message, and eleven students responded. From that point on, students responded almost every time we made an invitation. The following year, we gave invitations to faith from the very first weekly gathering. Eighty students came forward to make a first-time decision or a recommitment to follow Jesus wholeheartedly.

Soon afterward, students replaced campus ministers in giving talks at our weekly gatherings, and they invited their friends to follow Jesus. Not content to stop there, our student leaders started inviting their friends to follow Jesus in their small groups as well!

These events inspired other campus movements in San Diego to do the same kinds of things, and students responded to Jesus. We almost couldn't believe it; there had been a time when our county-wide ministry led only six students to faith in a given year. Within a decade, it grew to over six hundred.

But it's not just about the numbers. Ariel, a student at Cal State San Marcos, gave an invitation to faith in her sorority small group. Here's how she described it:

> As each word of prayer was being repeated after me, I felt God healing me of my own disbelief. I have seen God use others to lead in miraculous ways, but for God to use me like that was supernatural. In total, ten women made decisions in that one Bible study. My spirit was so humbled and just in awe to realize that God could use someone like me to speak truth into so many people's lives just like that. I broke down crying after the group left knowing that the God of the harvest was answering my prayers to see the Greek system transformed.

When was the last time we let Jesus call us to the edge of the cliff to take a leap of faith? What is Jesus calling us to? What would we do if failure or money wasn't an issue? Who could we talk with to find confirmation and wise counsel? What's keeping us from obeying our call today?

Recognize what God is saying.
Take your calls seriously.
Obey what you hear.
Jesus is waiting, and so is the world.

Discussion Questions

1. Who could you learn from that isn't connected to your particular tribe of faith, either currently or in history?
2. What is God calling you to audaciously ask for?
3. What call to revival is God asking you to be a part of?

Chapter Six

CONTENDING

Grit is living life like it's a marathon; not a sprint.
ANGELA LEE DUCKWORTH, "GRIT: THE POWER OF PASSION AND PERSEVERANCE"

I have fought the good fight, I have finished the race, I have kept the faith.
PAUL OF TARSUS, 2 TIMOTHY 4:7

In January of 1936, Bakht Singh felt called to lead a campaign of spiritual renewal in the town of Martinpur, India. At one time, this town had been strongly influenced by Christian missionaries who opened schools, hospitals, and colleges to serve the people.

But three generations later, the town had a notorious reputation for its disdain toward Christianity. Clearly, the spiritual influence of these early missionaries hadn't just waned, it had turned into contempt. It made Singh initially hesitant, but he heard a strong call to go.

His first gathering drew a surprisingly large crowd, but it wasn't a supportive one. Soon hecklers were mocking and laughing at him while he delivered his message, shouting, "Don't waste your time; nothing will happen here. Many have tried it and have gone on." In his travels, he had seen his fair share of challenges, but this was on a completely different level, one he hadn't encountered before.

It's hard to not ask, What would I have done here?

How do we respond when we come up against resistance and pushback, even with a call? We might be tempted to agree with the crowd and not waste our time. We might believe we've heard wrongly, that we've made a mistake in discernment. Perhaps we'd accuse ourselves of not being a good enough preacher. Maybe we'd seek a shift in strategy and take a different approach and find a strong worship leader or polish our digital branding. Perhaps we needed to pass out free food.

Instead, Singh stopped doing ministry. For four straight days, he didn't talk to anyone. He didn't even sleep. All he did was fast and pray. After those four days, he offered one last meeting and told people he'd be going away the following day.

As he closed in prayer, one man fell down in front of him. Others rolled on the ground, while others still pulled out their hair and beat their chests. In full repentance, they started to cry out to God for mercy. This went on until three in the morning.

These kinds of meetings continued for a whole week, and conviction spread from house to house, reconciling people to God and one another. Martinpur's change was dramatic, attracting people from surrounding villages to be a part of what the Holy Spirit was doing in the once-notorious town.

Revival had broken through.

But maybe Singh's actions sound a bit extreme. It's a bit much, no?

Yet, what if Singh knew something we have forgotten? Like the apostle Paul, Singh believed that breakthrough sometimes requires a good fight. To finish the race, we need to exercise our faith to its upper limits with grit and tenacity.

Singh knew how to contend.

Surveying the landscape of revival leadership in Scripture and church history, this same principle repeats itself over and over again.

Learning to Contend

Revivals require contenders who won't easily quit when the going gets tough. They won't back down when others say, "Give up!" They won't quiet down when others say, "Shut up." They won't let down until they know God has released them or given them the breakthrough.

Jesus has a lot to say to us about this principle of contending through an unlikely character:

> Then Jesus told his disciples a parable to show them that they should always pray and not give up. He said: "In a certain town there was a judge who neither feared God nor cared what people thought. And there was a widow in

that town who kept coming to him with the plea, 'Grant me justice against my adversary.'

"For some time he refused. But finally he said to himself, 'Even though I don't fear God or care what people think, yet because this widow keeps bothering me, I will see that she gets justice, so that she won't eventually come and attack me!'"

And the Lord said, "Listen to what the unjust judge says. And will not God bring about justice for his chosen ones, who cry out to him day and night? Will he keep putting them off? I tell you, he will see that they get justice, and quickly. However, when the Son of Man comes, will he find faith on the earth?"

Jesus could have drawn on the heroic exploits of David, Moses, or even Gideon. He didn't. And the judge is a man with prominence, position, and worldly power. This widow, however, is helpless, vulnerable, weak, and overlooked. She represents someone from the most powerless class of society, but she's a contender.

This story was meant to communicate one central practice that Jesus states right at the beginning: "to show them that they should always pray and not give up." Contending is about learning to pray in such a way as to not give up, precisely because perseverance requires us to fight against the voices and circumstances that pressure us to quit. Contending is about fighting with God's power and not with our own because we are called to always pray.

Consecration prepares us for the battle. Calling shows us where the battle is. Contending means learning how to fight until the battle is done.

Revival leaders anticipate resistance. Are we willing to contend for the breakthroughs Jesus has entrusted to us? When others reject us, when everything seems to be going against our expectations, when our prayers seem to be falling on deaf ears, and when the enemy whispers lies to our heart—"You are wasting your time!"—can we still contend?

Without contending, we might be surprised, like the Israelites with Moses, to find there are giants in the land of promise. When we don't expect a fight, we're more easily discouraged and deceived into thinking we've made a mistake about our calling. If we don't learn how to fight, then we'll be exhausted and burned out, doubling down and fighting in our own strength. Having been consecrated, we might be tempted to depend on past spiritual experiences with God while forgoing fresh infusions of power from the Spirit.

Consecration is digging the well and finding the deep artisan spring of God's Spirit flowing. Contending is learning to live in that spring, even as it grows deeper and wider into a river that sweeps us off our feet and carries us beyond our control.

In contending, consecration is not just our past but our lifestyle.

Contending is essential for revival leaders. It's fighting with conviction in God's ability and desire to bring the breakthrough. If we want to train to fight with conviction and contend for works of God, there are five insights into contending that we'll need to understand first.

Put In Effort but Don't Earn

First, understanding the difference between earning and effort is an indispensable lesson for the revival contender. Seeking God for revival is getting into a fight we can't win on our own. The breakthrough of revival comes to us completely by the grace of God. There is nothing we can do to earn or deserve or manufacture revival by our goodness, efforts, or desires.

Why then are we talking about contending, when it seems the battle belongs to God?

Don't assume that grace is opposed to effort. Effort isn't trying to earn what only grace can bestow. Dallas Willard clarifies it this way: "Grace is not opposed to effort, it is opposed to earning. Earning is an attitude. Effort is an action."

Willard's distinction between attitude and action is crucial. Our attitude is made up of feelings and thoughts. Our attitudes are significant internal motivating forces that direct our actions and choices to the circumstances in our life. Earning is the attitude that says, "It's all up to me."

At the top of the U curve, our attitude is usually positive and optimistic. Is that based on our confidence to earn breakthrough or on God's faithfulness to do more than we could ever imagine?

At the bottom of the U curve, the heat of the crisis exposes our true attitudes. The earning attitude puts the breakthrough squarely on our shoulders: our effort, our plans, our timing, our process, our desires, our hard work. The earning attitude pressures us with anxiety and pride to work harder. It taunts our pride, saying, "God helps those who help themselves," which, for the record, is not anywhere in the Bible.

But once we've reached the limits of our own strength, then the earning attitude turns on us to condemn us. It disheartens us with fear and self-pity, saying things like, "See, you were such a naive fool to seek God for this breakthrough."

What motivates our efforts matters.

For the persistent widow, her effort wasn't motivated by her confidence to win the fight, but rather it was in God's grace to give her what she couldn't earn or deserve. Jesus' portrayal of the judge captures the worst caricature of God in times of crisis: a miserly, disinterested old man who needs to be badgered into helping. But as it goes, if someone like this judge eventually capitulates, how much more will our grace-oriented, heavenly Father respond to our persistence?

Paul described the vital role of grace-empowered effort in his own life: "He is the one we proclaim, admonishing and teaching everyone with all wisdom, so that we may present everyone fully mature in Christ. To this end I strenuously contend with all the energy Christ so powerfully works in me."

By faith in God's grace, Paul's life was energized by a supernatural power that enabled him to "strenuously contend" where others, leaning on their own strength, would have failed. Because Paul had an attitude of trust in God's grace to give him everything he needed, he was able to say, "I have learned the secret of being content in any and every situation, whether well fed or hungry, whether living in plenty or in want."

That is the power of God's grace. Grace can energize our efforts with enduring strength. It can ground our expectancy in God's ability to accomplish something. There is freedom in knowing that we don't have what it takes on our own, and we can count on God meeting us at the very moment we come to the end of ourselves.

In fact, God often waits for us to get to the end of ourselves before he chooses to break through to ensure that we are grace centered.

In this way, contending frees all of us.

Cry Out

The next practice in contending is learning the importance of crying out to God. Jesus exhorts at the end of the parable, "And will not God bring about justice for his chosen ones, who *cry out* to him day and night?"

This is both an invitation and a promise. The invitation is to find enough courage to get in touch with our deeper longing for God's help to break through. It takes strength to resist the voices of fear and worst-case scenarios that seek to kill that desire in us.

Revival contenders have to choose to fight against the onslaught of discouragement on the one hand and self-reliance on the other. For this reason, it's hard emotional work to maintain hope in God and stoke the flame of our desire when things aren't going the way we expected. In honesty, it's just easier and more comfortable to give in to our despair and resignation, and thus fall into the loop of despair.

Going back to the widow, how many times did she entreat the judge only to find cold indifference? We don't know the exact number, but it's easy to get the picture that she was at it for an extended time. For a long while, her pleas fell on deaf ears and an unresponsive heart.

But underneath the firm, resolute exterior, something inside the judge was bending and giving way to her constant pressure. When we cry out to God, we're putting pressure on the spiritual forces of evil. We're also putting ourselves in a position to wait on his timing and perspective.

Crying out to God means persistent, whole-hearted praying, where we unload the full freight of our hope onto him, withholding none of it for our plans and strategies. God's promise to those who cry out to him is that they will not be overlooked.

The enemy of our souls wants to keep us quiet and keep the struggle locked deep inside. It can feel foolish, or worse yet, forced. Or it just makes some of us uncomfortable.

But the Spirit will often inspire us to cry out, to release the burden in order to find our strength in him. And this kind of whole-hearted praying is recorded throughout the book of Psalms:

> All night long I flood my bed with weeping and drench my couch with tears....
>
> Evening, morning and noon I cry out in distress, and he hears my voice....

> Lord, you are the God who saves me; day and night I cry out to you.

Off the coast of Scotland lies a diverse archipelago called the Hebrides. It contains some of the oldest rocks in Europe, and consists of more than 136 islands—of which fifteen are inhabited. Although high in latitude, the Gulf Stream keeps these islands rather temperate, and from 1948 to 1952, they played host to the Hebrides Revival.

In November 1949, on the island of Lewis, two women in their eighties—one of them blind—were burdened by the spiritual state of their church. Not a single young person was a part of their parish, so the women started to pray twice a week, often from ten o'clock at night to three or four o'clock in the morning.

As they prayed, one of them received a vision of their church packed with young people. They called their parish minister about it and challenged him to host his own prayer meeting at the same times—Tuesday and Friday nights. He accepted and started to pray with seven men.

After a month and a half, a young deacon in the church read Psalm 24 while they prayed in the barn: "He that has clean hands and a pure heart who has not lifted up his soul unto vanity or sworn deceitfully. He shall receive the blessing (not a blessing, but the blessing) of the Lord." Then he closed his Bible, and looking down, he said words straight from his heart: "It seems to me to be so much humbug to be praying as we are praying, to be waiting as we are waiting, if we ourselves are not rightly related to God."

Then he lifted his two hands. It would be hard not to hear the tremble in his voice, as he cried out, "God, are my hands clean? Is my heart pure?" Then he fell into a trance.

Conviction hit the room. "A God-sent revival must ever be related to holiness." And the power of God swept in. Later, at a nearby dance hall, the presence of God would move in so dramatically that the music stopped, and in minutes the hall emptied of its one hundred or so young people, and they all went to church. Soon after, eight hundred—with many young people—poured into the church and prayed until four in the morning.

And the revival would last for three more years.

Revivals, both personally and corporately, depend on this kind of praying, because revivals depend on God's power, not our own.

Pray Day and Night

In the parable, Jesus challenges us not only to cry out, but to cry out "day and night." Sometimes our contending will be measured in days or weeks, and at other times it will be measured in months or years. Building our prayer stamina so that we can cry out day and night is the third critical practice in contending for revival.

For example, Roberts personally prayed every night for almost eleven years to see the revival that broke out across Wales and spread out to the ends of the earth. For many of those years, he also maintained this commitment by attending prayer meetings each weeknight.

We might not imitate Roberts's nightly schedule, but how could we learn to pray over the long haul without giving up? For many, praying for even ten to twenty minutes a day can seem too difficult to maintain. How can we develop the kind of grit that will allow us to run a prayer marathon instead of a sprint?

Running a marathon is daunting. The messenger who ran the first marathon, delivering a message by foot across the 26.2 miles from Marathon to Athens—he died! We can't just do it. But with training, we can incrementally develop stamina and strength, avoiding injury and complete discouragement.

In prayer we can also train so that we don't become completely discouraged in contending. What if we committed to praying for an hour daily for the revival God has called us to contend for? How would we begin engaging with that kind of commitment? If we are like most people and find the prospect of praying daily for an hour to be overwhelming, then consider the following training schedule:

Open your schedule. First, in the same way a runner preparing for a marathon commits to a daily exercise regimen focused on achieving a marathon, commit to daily scheduled prayer. Open your calendar and get ready to be concrete about when you'll pray.

I (Ryan) have learned the hard way; if something doesn't get in my calendar, it doesn't get done. It's not glamorous, but it works. I treat my prayer times with Jesus as real appointments. I even have my phone alert me to pause and pray during the day.

Do mornings and evenings. Second, break your daily prayer time into two segments of time: an early part and a late part of the day. Bookending your day in specific prayer will keep this topic on your mind while spacing out prayer sessions so you don't have to try and do it all at once.

For my mornings, I focus on Scripture reading, silence, meditation, and then worship. But in the evenings, I prefer to go for a walk while praying.

It's a great way for me to unwind from all the restless energy of the workday. I love to talk out loud with Jesus, imagining him walking right beside me, stride for stride.

Start small. Third, set each session for five minutes. With two sessions, you're already at ten minutes a day! You could make them longer, but the point is to set it at a length that feels sustainable at first. Don't stretch yet. If you begin with something more herculean, you'll likely become inconsistent, which will kill your motivation. Start easy, but daily.

I remember when I was in my early twenties, committing myself to a bench at a local park to pray for three hours in one sitting. I was able to keep this up three times a week for a heroic two weeks, and then I gave up entirely. After that I only prayed in fits and starts. I had a go-big-or-go-home attitude that, in the end, made it hard to persevere. I have learned the sobering lesson that it's hard to pray when your rear end is numb.

Build gradually. After a week, increase your total daily prayer time by five more minutes. You're only adding two and a half minutes to each session. Then decide—increase it every week or every two weeks? Scale it according to your urgency and schedule. In six or twelve weeks, depending on what you choose, you'll be praying for an hour a day.

Back in January, I started practicing silent meditation—a discipline that's particularly hard for me as a verbal processor—before reading Scripture in order to improve my sensitivity to God's voice. I began with only five minutes. My pride urged me to go for twenty minutes, but experience and humility told me to keep it simple. Now, four months later, I have incrementally built up my listening capacity to between twenty and thirty minutes. My mind, spirit, and even my body have built up endurance for that kind of sustained attention.

Have rest days and long days. When you train for a marathon, you're supposed to have weekly rest days and one long run day. Rest allows your body to adjust to the added strain. The long run days, however, allow you to prepare for the next level of distance without overwhelming yourself. Plan two rest days each week when you will not schedule time to pray for the breakthrough. If the desire comes to pray on those days, feel free to intercede if you like, but don't push yourself to do it out of obligation or guilt. Remember, what motivates your effort matters. For the long day, pick a time when you can double the period you spend praying on a single day. So if you are praying a total of ten minutes a session, then pick a day that week to pray twenty minutes in one session, and build accordingly.

Fridays and Saturdays are my days off. So while the kids are at school, the house is quiet and a perfect place for extended periods of prayer without fearing interruptions. Although when I used to take my long days on Sundays—before I worked as a pastor—I loved that my kids would spontaneously come into my bedroom and join me for a small portion of my prayer time.

Print it out. Make yourself a schedule, print it out, and pin it up where you can see it every day—to both remind you and encourage you. It's exhilarating to see yourself grow and move toward a goal that you never thought you could achieve. Even more, God himself is delighted by this kind of intentionality and committed pursuit. Love is always intentional, so God loves it when we come after him, offering our time and our hearts.

My friend Abner finds tremendous traction this way. He writes his prayer schedule and pins it up for the family to see. When he fulfills his commitment for the day, he puts a sticker on it. His family can see his prayer patterns and cheer him on. There's powerful accountability when your six-year-old asks you, "Papa, why didn't you get a sticker yesterday?"

Go Hungry for God

John Piper makes a direct link between fasting and revival. He writes, "There is in our own day a growing sense among many that the rediscovery of fasting as a penitential heart-cry to God for revival might be the means God would use to awaken and reform his church.... The course of history has been changed repeatedly through fasting and prayer."

How does the practice of fasting help us contend for revival? We've been talking marathons, but there are also times to sprint. Consistency is essential, but intensity matters as well.

Intensity is the sudden burst of energy, a moment of extreme engagement. In an endurance race, steady pacing takes up most of the race. But to pass an opponent, a runner needs moments of acceleration. And when closing in on the finish line, even-keeled runners will break into an all-out sprint to win the race.

Contending for revival requires we integrate both consistency and intensity, steady pacing and sprinting, endurance as well as power. Don't substitute one for the other.

If daily prayer is the marathon, fasting is the sprint. It's a powerful focusing tool to increase our intensity. Revival leaders need to guard their intensity and zeal because the world is constantly working to distract, diminish, dissipate, and extinguish our intensity for the things of heaven. "The greatest enemy of hunger for God is not poison but apple pie," writes Piper.

How does fasting help protect and intensify our spiritual hunger, stoking the fire in us to new levels of fervency? Think about how much of our day revolves around food. Abstaining from food disrupts our schedule, our social interactions at the meal table, and our bodies.

Fasting for one meal can have this effect, but prolonged fasts are my favorite. When fasting for more than a day, the disruption is inescapable. The gnawing in my stomach arrests my attention and brings me back to what I am seeking God for. At first the hunger I feel is an unwelcome guest—a badgering, nagging occupant I wish I could get rid of.

In this case, the hunger in me is like the widow from the parable, harassing and attacking me with her cause until I yield more of my heart than I've wanted to give. I am the unjust judge, resisting God's passionate claim on me. It's no longer my hunger for food but God's hunger for breakthrough and revival that is coming after me until I yield.

Yet, once I embrace it, my hunger becomes a friend who seeks to nudge me back into focus. I would find myself piggybacking on the hunger pangs, saying to myself, *God, I want to hunger for you like I hunger for that cheeseburger. God, as much as I want food right now, I want you even more.*

Fasting harnesses the raw energy of our physical hunger to focus us toward God and his purposes. Through this kind of focus, fasting increases our capacity to receive greater infusions of God's glory and power. An example from Charles Finney's life illustrates this point:

> Sometimes I would find myself, in a great measure, empty of this power. I would go out and visit, and find that I made no saving impression. I would exhort and pray with the same result. I would then set apart a day for private fasting and prayer, fearing that this power had departed from me, and would inquire anxiously after the reason of this apparent emptiness. After

humbling myself, and crying out for help, the power would return upon me with all its freshness. This has been the experience of my life.

When Singh or Finney came up against roadblocks, resistance, or failure, they didn't back down, work harder, or become insecure. Instead, they contended with fasting. In our physical hunger and weakness, God's power is perfected in us because it puts us in touch with the deeper spiritual truth of our helplessness apart from God's mercy.

Fasting isn't a formula that guarantees revival. It definitely isn't a way for us to earn favor with God. It's not a quid pro quo arrangement: "God, I'm sacrificing so much. Now you owe me!" It doesn't entitle us to anything nor does it manipulate God into acting in our favor.

It's a way to focus, a way to contend for revival.

Retreat to Advance

Think about a boxing match. What comes to mind? Muscular pugilists, bobbing and weaving? Fancy footwork? Jabs and hooks? Perhaps the sound of the crowd, shouting and cheering for their contender?

But it's easy to miss the moment the bell is rung to end a round. When it's struck, boxers head to their corners and sit on their stools. Sweat is toweled off. Cuts are sewn. Salts try to revive.

Every boxer needs to rest to stay in the fight. To contend for revival, we need to learn to rest.

Learning to retreat and rest is the final essential practice in contending for revival. We cannot always be in fight mode. The psalmist writes:

> In vain you rise early
> and stay up late,
> toiling for food to eat—
> for he grants sleep to those he loves....
> They will not be put to shame
> when they contend with their opponents in court.

In essence, the psalm is saying, "Those who learn to rest in the Lord will not be put to shame; when they contend, they will have God in their corner."

Understanding the role of rest and retreat is essential to fighting for the long haul. Failing to understand this lesson, we become vulnerable to workaholism. The truth is, when we overwork and toil, rising early and staying up late, it's likely we've lost touch with God's power.

Wait. Didn't Jesus tell us to cry out day and night? Didn't Singh go without sleeping for four days while fasting and praying?

Sure, there will be times where we do a short sprint in the marathon. But that's different from having ongoing patterns of late-night work. Singh's praying and fasting was for a few days, but if he had repeated this pattern on a weekly basis without rest, he probably would have been trusting more in his prayers than in God.

Overworking means disregarding the appropriate boundaries of rest and sleep to the point of hurting your health and relationships. Sleep is an act of faith that God is in charge, not you. In revival leadership, retreat isn't optional.

Revival leaders in history have burned out from failing to recognize that overworking ignores God's grace. They often have an entrepreneurial spirit, so by temperament they can throw themselves completely and wholeheartedly into their work. And if it's for God, all the more reason for sacrifice, right?

Roberts suffered from what appears to be a kind of work addiction, arguably resulting in his nervous breakdown and withdrawal from public ministry after only two years of revival leadership. We've spoken with many ministry leaders who have thrown themselves into tireless service, only to find themselves emotionally bankrupt and unable to recover their joy in ministry, like a used-up battery that has lost its charge.

Some biographers of revival leaders seem to laud this unhealthy work ethic rather than recognize it as a fault to be cautioned against. Maybe it's this very problem that has made us wary of engaging with revival. Rest assured, literally. There is a different way.

Jesus himself often withdrew to his corner to be alone with his Father. After a late night of preaching and healing in Capernaum, Mark records Jesus withdrawing early in the morning to pray. When his disciples find him, they're frantic: "Everyone is looking for you!" Jesus responded, "Let us go somewhere else—to the nearby villages—so I can preach there also. That is why I have come."

Retreating into his Father's presence allowed Jesus to maintain perspective and remain faithful to his calling. As a result, Jesus continued his advance into the surrounding villages of Galilee, and ultimately this pattern sustained him all the way to the cross. We see him again, retreating into his Father's presence before entering the "ring" at Golgotha.

If Jesus had to retreat to advance, then it'd be fair to say that we do too. Yet how many leaders have mistaken their ability to forgo rest as a mark of zeal for God's call? How many leaders fail to retreat out of guilt, feeling they are being selfish? How many families have needlessly suffered from an absent parent, all in the name of passion for God's call? And how many times has exhaustion or moral failure struck down leaders because they were unwilling to contend using the power provided through rest and retreat?

Busyness can become a mask to cover up the painful, dark places in our souls that need attention from the Spirit. Rest allows space for the Spirit to address our wounds and losses. If neglected, these dark places—filled with feelings of doubt, disappointment, and even despair—can leave us vulnerable to greater kinds of failures.

Resting, sleep, sabbath, sabbaticals, and retreats are ways we accept our inherent limitations as created beings. Rest honors God precisely because it recognizes that we are not God. Rest is an act of faith that God is the one who energizes us for the fight.

For me (James), these are some of the rhythms that currently sustain me. But they'll change with the seasons, depending on what God is leading me to and what I may need. Daily, I pray four times a day because I need that kind of sustenance to match the spiritual responsibilities God has given me. Weekly, I pray and reflect on Monday mornings to prepare for the week. Quarterly, I take a retreat day and meet with my spiritual director, who can point out the ways Jesus is working in my life. And annually, I find myself reflecting and praying with Benedictine monks in the high desert for three days.

It's the rhythms of retreat and advance that have helped me stay grounded. The Lord knows I need them.

Putting these five practices together, we contend. Bakht contended when he faced opposition. Roberts prayed nightly for a decade. Finney contended when he felt a season of powerlessness.

And if we're to seek revival, we are also invited to contend.

Discussion Questions

1. In what ways are you tempted to earn something through your spiritual efforts?
2. Which of the five contending practices connected with you the most? Why?

3. In what ways is God calling you to contend?

Chapter Seven

CHARACTER

This is true humility: not thinking less of ourselves, but thinking of ourselves less.
RICK WARREN, *THE PURPOSE DRIVEN LIFE*

For all those who exalt themselves will be humbled, and those who humble themselves will be exalted.
JESUS OF NAZARETH, LUKE 18:14

The prophetic gifts were getting to my head.

It had only been a couple of days since I (James) first received the gift of prophecy after throwing out those CDs, and I had been offered prophetic words throughout my waking hours. Unfortunately, most of the words I had were exposing someone else's sin.

I'd walk up to someone—friend or stranger—and tell them what sin they were struggling with. And I'd do it in an affected way, doubling over as if lightly punched in the stomach with a voice more akin to Yoda than anything else. And surprisingly, or alarmingly, the word would often be right on. Then we'd pray, and not helping my pride in any way, they'd feel like they had met the Lord.

The next day, as I sat down for Sunday service, I thought I had a sense of the preacher's hidden sins.

I felt like a superhero.

And as someone who was barely into his twenties, the rush was intoxicating. I felt powerful. As the hours went on, I felt more and more right about what I was doing.

At this time, I was also the leader of our faith community at my alma mater. We had leadership meetings on Sunday nights, and before the meeting began, I saw my campus minister, Soong-Chan Rah. He'd been away, visiting the Airport Vineyard in Toronto. It was the days before cell phones, and I wanted to tell him everything that had happened in the last couple of days. But before I could get a word out, he handed me two tapes for training on prophecy.

"How did you know?" I asked.

He just smiled knowingly. "I know."

Then we turned to our leadership team meeting. I shared about what had happened to me the last Friday, and by fiat, I ditched the agenda to call a spontaneous prayer meeting. As we prayed, I had the sense that God wanted to do something for a particular person on our team. I pointed at him and said that he had to confess his sins.

And as crazy as that sounds in the telling, he actually did.

When Soong-Chan started to pray for that person, I just stopped him in the middle of his prayer and said that he was doing it all wrong. He was praying the wrong things.

In his humility, he didn't stop me.

In my cockiness, I kept going.

And sure, that person felt a deep, abiding sense of peace and joy—and couldn't stop laughing either. With his arms around our shoulders, we had to half-carry him back to his dorm.

In it all, I acted out of pure instinct, without care for how I was treating other people. It was often brusque, aggressive, and absent of love and care. I was strident.

I'm thankful that within the next few hours, two things happened that drew me up.

First, leaders from another fellowship came for advice. They had heard the ways God had gifted me, so they wanted to ask me to ask God for direction about their fellowship. I'm thankful that I had the wherewithal then to say that they shouldn't be asking me. They should ask God.

But that was weird.

Even if I were gaining spiritual authority quickly on campus, that shouldn't keep people from connecting with God themselves, right?

The second incident was more humbling. I gave a prophetic word, saying that someone else was praying for us at that moment. Later, when said someone arrived at our meeting, we asked him if he had prayed for us.

"No. Why?"

That was the first time in forty-eight hours that something I "prophesied" was confirmed to be wrong. And if I could be wrong about that one thing, then I could be wrong about many things.

I could be wrong about anything.

So I pulled back.

When I later listened to the tapes Soong-Chan had given me, they were about how prophets needed to test all things and express all things through the fruit of the Spirit. Oh, I really needed those tapes. They were given to me to address my character.

A friend of mine once said a funny thing about marriages that stuck with me over the decades. He said that 90 percent of his marriage brought out the very best in him. He couldn't imagine loving or serving anyone more.

But 10 percent of it brought out the very worst in him. He'd never treated anyone so poorly.

Revivals could be the same way, couldn't they? They can bring out the best in people and our faith communities, but for some, they can also bring out the worst.

As history shows, a strong move of God is often accompanied by a commensurate backlash from spiritual opposition. As you push the front lines of spiritual conflict, you get stuff in return.

Some of the stuff is overt opposition. Other times, the flush of excitement brings to light the flaws that we were able to hide before. A number burn out, while others escape through infidelity or addiction.

In his study of thousands of leaders over their lifetimes, Bobby Clinton says that only one of three leaders finishes well. He highlights six barriers that cause leaders to fail: improper handling of finances, abuse of power, inordinate pride, illicit sexual relationships, family problems, and plateauing. All deal with character in some way.

So if we want revival to thrive and spread, our character is a big part of the equation.

An Epidemic of Contempt

When seeking revival, it's easy to become strident. If unchecked, it can lead to dangerous and extreme views.

In Jesus' day, there were others, beside him, who sought revival. They were called Pharisees. They were willing to be living examples, set apart from the world, so that God would show his favor on a nation in exile. Israel was under Roman rule, and that, according to their covenant with God, must be because Israel was somehow disobedient and unrepentant. If they could turn the nation back to God, perhaps he would throw off their Roman oppressors and reestablish the sovereign kingdom of Israel.

So they fasted. If there were rules in Torah, they would create extra rules so they wouldn't even come close to breaking anything in Torah. They would strictly obey everything that was written, and then some.

They sought revival, and they were unbearable.

On the other side of the social spectrum, tax collectors were sellouts, traitors, and compromisers who allied with the Roman Empire for financial gain at the expense of their kinsmen. They were good-for-nothings. Don't even be seen talking with one, unless you also want to become unclean.

They didn't seek revival. They were going to get rich or die trying. Loyalties, be damned.

Knowing this background, Jesus told a story about a Pharisee and a tax collector. The Pharisee thanked God for not being like the tax collector praying next to him: "God, I thank you that I am not like other people—robbers, evildoers, adulterers—or even like this tax collector." He praised his own giving and spiritual prowess.

It sounds obtuse to us today, but in Jesus' day, the Pharisee's prayer would've been seen as a good thing. Of course holy people thanked God for their piety; their holiness is from God. It was a common prayer, but Jesus would turn it on its head and expose it for what it was.

In the heart of this revival leader, something is amiss. The narrator won't let us miss it. He drops the purpose of this story in the preamble: "To some who were confident of their own righteousness and looked down on everyone else, Jesus told this parable."

Jesus wanted to address their contempt.

Here's one definition of contempt: the feeling that a person or a thing is beneath consideration, worthless, or deserving scorn. It's the weapon of pride. If pride makes you think you're better than others, then contempt is feeling that others are worse. One puffs up, the other destroys.

Psychologist John Gottman could predict after being with a couple for fifteen minutes whether their marriage would survive with 90 percent accuracy. What was he looking for?

Contempt.

And he could see it in the roll of an eye, the cluck of a tongue. It didn't take much.

And these days, we see the ways that contempt has filled the airwaves, corroded our political processes, blasted apart communities and countries. No one is listening anymore, especially if we disagree. And it's a poison.

All of us need to watch ourselves in this area of contempt. It's where our passion for God can turn into stony religionism. When others don't consecrate themselves as we do, when they don't share our passion for the calling we carry, when they don't agree with us, reject us, criticize us, patronize us, or dismiss our longing for revival, it's tempting to allow contempt into our hearts.

It's tempting to think we're the true believers. Soothing our wounded egos, assuaging our self-doubt, contempt tells us lies: No one gets it like we do. We're special. God is revealing things to us that they just can't grasp. They're so spiritually dry. It's up to us to change this group and be a prophetic voice. The leaders sure aren't going to do anything. We just need to go to a different church and find people who think like us.

If they were truly spiritual they would—you name it! Pray, worship, fast, read, serve, protest like me. You haven't consecrated as I have. You don't know how long I've contended!

Contempt is dangerous not just because of what it does to others and our relationships but because it hurts our souls. It makes us feel right, and everyone else wrong. So, with a hardened heart, no other voices matter but ours alone.

That's when the revival leader becomes the Pharisee.

As with many young leaders, Evan Roberts of the Welsh Revival mistook his youthful energy to be inexhaustible. But soon his inability to stop and rest led to an exaggerated sense of self-importance. His earlier tendencies of speaking less and giving freedom in meetings gave way to more domination in meetings, to more control.

It really unraveled when he measured the spiritual temperature of an entire congregation through his own emotional and temperamental state. He would stop the meeting and declare that someone in the room was obstructing the work of the Spirit just because he couldn't feel the Spirit in the room.

One author describes it this way: "Evan himself began to describe every grumble or whispered remark and every challenging question as the work of Satan. The man who had once delighted in a bit of humor was now easily upset by a grin or whisper." His winsome, childlike wonder had hardened into cynical contempt.

How do we know if we've landed deeply into contempt? Ask yourself these questions: Do you regularly push to get the last word? Do you fantasize about proving yourself in an argument? Do you talk about people behind their backs? Do you work to steer the sympathies of others toward yourself and against others? Do you give in to the urge to promote yourself?

If you answered yes to many of these questions, then contempt may have a claim on your heart.

The Test of Humility

The antidote? Jesus commends the tax collector for showing us a different way: "The tax collector stood at a distance. He would not even look up to heaven, but beat his breast and said, 'God, have mercy on me, a sinner.'"

This man, according to Jesus, will be exalted because of his humility.

The South African revival leader and devotional writer Andrew Murray described humility as the "root of every virtue" and pride—the absence of humility—as the "root of every sin and evil."

Humility isn't self-abasement. It's not saying how horrible we are. It's about self-forgetfulness. Pastor Rick Warren puts it another way: "This is true humility: not thinking less of ourselves, but thinking of ourselves less."

We think of ourselves less because humility has us preoccupied and smitten by the One on whom our hope truly rests. The effect of placing our attention on God is that it places our view of our self in proper perspective, and along with that everyone else around us is brought into proper perspective.

One test of our humility is in the answer to this question: How do you take criticism?

Humility allows us to hear criticism and weigh it thoughtfully without the snap reaction of fear and insecurity. Solomon shared a proverb along these lines: "Those who disregard discipline despise themselves, but the one who heeds correction gains understanding."

Humility doesn't shrink back from conflict, but it's always respectful, quick to listen, and slow to speak. Author David Brooks gives us a good start, describing it as "freedom from the need to prove you are superior all the time.... Humility is the awareness that there's a lot you don't know and that a lot of what you think you know is distorted or wrong."

Humility does more. It emanates a beauty that attracts people to its warm light. Take for example Brooks's description of a person imbued with this inner quality:

> They radiate a moral joy. They answer softly when challenged harshly. They are silent when unfairly abused. They are dignified when others try to humiliate them, restrained when others try to provoke them. But they get things done. They perform acts of sacrificial service with the same modest everyday spirit they would display if they were just getting the groceries. They are not thinking about what impressive work they are doing.

Wouldn't we want to be like that?

When we meet people marked with this rare quality, it's hard not to admire them and even envy them. That's because the calmness and quietness in the humbled soul gives off the aroma of true spiritual authority.

The reactive, defensive person, despite their puffed out chest and vociferous arguments, betrays their insecurity. We can all sense it. We are less persuaded by the one who pushes hard to convince us.

The U curve is fundamentally a road to character transformation through humility. The crisis of faith is in fact a crucible of character perfectly designed by God to deepen our humility. Our faith can only rise as high as the depth of our humility will support. The higher the building, the deeper the foundation must be. The forging of humility is fundamental to the maturing of our character and essential to the journey of seeking God for revival.

Revival leadership invariably takes us on a path of confrontation with the status quo, and that means our character will be tested by both the praise we receive and the rejection we suffer. When people misunderstand, disagree, and push back at us because of the calling God has given us, will we become embittered? When others praise us for our passion and single us out as a prophetic voice of God, will we become prideful? How we respond matters a great deal.

Count Nikolaus Ludwig von Zinzendorf's humility was put to the test throughout his leadership of the Moravian community in eighteenth-century Europe.

Protestant refugees from Bohemia and Moravia had taken residence on the Count's large estate in Berthelsdorf, Germany. It wasn't long before hundreds of families were living on his property. This community of Protestant refugees became the kernel of the Moravian movement.

Yet early on, despite all his kindness and generosity, some who were jealous of Zinzendorf's leadership began spreading vicious slander about Zinzendorf, even calling him "the beast out of the abyss." Skepticism and division fractured the community, not only in their relationship with Zinzendorf but also with each other.

To make matters worse, government leadership heard about the conflict on his estate and put pressure on him to kick the refugees off his property. It was certainly within Zinzendorf's right to do so, but humility guided him along a wiser path.

Instead, he visited each family over the course of three days and three nights in a row. He kept visiting, except to sleep a few hours at night. He contended for a breakthrough in the conflict by earnestly praying by himself and with the families, working tirelessly to restore unity.

Zinzendorf didn't focus his visits on defending his reputation or attacking the men who slandered him. He heard what people had to say, and then he turned their focus back to Jesus. He preached about the necessity of unity, the importance of allegiance to Jesus above all, and he led them in an all-night prayer vigil. The people found firm footing once again on the stable ground of Zinzendorf's humility, paving the way for the Holy Spirit.

The breakthrough of the Spirit was palpable, reminiscent of Pentecost. Men and women were brought to their knees in tearful confession and surrender as they embraced and forgave one another.

Later, he was slandered by the aristocracy, the town guilds, and the Lutheran church, all who were quick to believe lies about his theology and practices. They branded Zinzendorf an outlaw, an outcast, a dreamer, a fanatic, and even unsaved. Eventually he was exiled from Germany in 1736. Even then, he didn't become bitter or discouraged, vowing, "I will pray daily for my superiors and persecutors."

Zinzendorf chose to see his exile as God's providence opening a door for worldwide influence. He traveled wide, planting Moravian communities in the Baltics, the Netherlands, the West Indies, and even in New York and Pennsylvania. Zinzendorf's humility won souls throughout the world and eventually the trust of his fiercest detractors. After ten years of banishment, he was allowed to return home to Herrnhut.

Humility is persuasive because it serves as a channel for the grace of God to soften people's hearts and makes a smooth path for the Spirit to do the convincing.

What if this were the story for more churches that have ended in painful splits?

More than ever, as we seek God for revival, we need to allow God to humble us so that we can become the channels of his reviving grace.

Be Open to Wonder

After the story about the Pharisee and the tax collector, Luke shows Jesus' humility in action.

People wanted their children to be with Jesus, blessed by his hands, but the disciples weren't having any of it. To the modern reader, that might seem weird. Aren't children great? Why wouldn't they want him to be with children?

Children, like widows, however, represented the lowest status of society. Hanging out with them would only take their own status down a few notches.

It wouldn't look good for the movement to embrace lower-class folks, so Jesus' disciples didn't want their rabbi sullied by relating to—blecch!—children.

Yet Jesus didn't care about that. He called the children to him and taught the haughty disciples about the nature of the kingdom —that the kingdom belongs to people like the children. He sums it up this way: "Truly I tell you, anyone who will not receive the kingdom of God like a little child will never enter it."

What does that mean? How can we be children again?

My (James's) five-year-old daughter is sheer walking and breathing delight. She is fascinated by her life around her, investigating and asking questions. At any moment, she's ready to dance for us. All of life is full to her, and she can't wait to take in more of it. She is alive with wonder.

Contempt is the opposite. It no longer seeks to soak up the goodness that surrounds us and is content to put up walls and peek down at everything else from its lofty tower. It no longer tastes, no longer asks questions. Contempt kills wonder.

And the kingdom was meant to be alive with wonder.

What if we actually live in an enchanted world, full of spirit and meaning, but we're closed off to it because contempt has consumed our soul? What if we're missing what life can offer because we look down at everything else around us? If we find ourselves no longer able to tap into awe and wonder, then we've allowed contempt to strangle our souls.

That's the thing, when we judge the Pharisees, we become one. That's how contempt works.

Jesus, instead, shows another way. Though he was God, he came to earth as a baby. Although he could take the world by force, he gave up his life on the cross so that the penalty and power of sin could die with him. On the third day, God raised him up from the dead so that a new life and a new world are possible.

It has always been the humble way. Paul writes:

> He humbled himself

by becoming obedient to death—
even death on a cross!
Therefore God exalted him to the highest place
and gave him the name that is above every name.

And through his humility, a movement bearing his name would change the world.

Character grounds the other revival practices. The maturity of our character determines the level of our consecration. The depth of our character supports the height of our calling. And the strength of our character sustains the endurance of our contending.

Character bolsters revival. Without character, revival grinds to a halt because leadership flows out of who we are.

My (James's) wife's name is Jinhee. Her name in Korean means "truth" and "joy." And over the past nineteen years, she's been a tremendous source of joy to me. But when I blow it, she is also a herald of truth. She offers up a mirror to my soul, and when I'm listening, I get a better picture of who I am and a clearer path of who God wants me to be. Add the voice of my spiritual director, my confessor, my ministry colleagues, and other close friends, and I find I have the community around me that can speak truth into my life, to help me not go off the rails.

Throughout the U curve process, the Spirit of God is refining our character as in a refiner's fire, preparing us to live with humility and faith at the new normal the breakthrough is intended to produce.

Consecration prepares us for revival leadership. Calling gives us direction in revival leadership. Contending gives us the perseverance to keep pursuing revival leadership, while character helps us remain qualified for revival leadership. These four practices help us experience revival in our souls, and prepare us for the revival to come.

But seeking God for revival can tempt us to take ourselves too seriously. Don't let your character quench revival. As we seek God for a breakthrough in the world, we must pay attention to the Spirit's work to bring a breakthrough of Christ's character in us.

Discussion Questions

1. Is there someone or a group of people you hold in contempt? How can you ask God for forgiveness and freedom in this area?
2. Who could you ask for more feedback about your character and leadership?
3. What rhythms would allow you to learn one new thing daily from others, especially from people who are not like you?

PART THREE
LEADING REVIVAL

Chapter Eight

ALL PLAY

Everyone gets to play.
JOHN WIMBER, *EVERYONE GETS TO PLAY*

Now to each one the manifestation of the Spirit is given for the common good.
PAUL OF TARSUS, 1 CORINTHIANS 12:7

Campus by the Sea is a retreat center nestled in the foothills of Catalina Island, and it edges right up to the Pacific. It's so secluded that no roads lead to it; we arrived by boat. It dropped us off on a wooden pier, and then we dragged our luggage across a rocky beach lined with palm trees until we hit the main dirt path that ran right up through the middle of camp. Most of the cabins don't have electricity, and the walls don't reach up to the ceiling.

Every night, as we slept, cold ocean air filled our lungs.

In the evening, I (James) gave a talk on the rich young ruler out of Luke 18, asking students from all over San Diego County to give up the "one thing" to follow Jesus. Worship had been electric, and it had already been a wonder-filled night, infused with God's Spirit.

Our custom is to help students follow Jesus in a public way by asking them to stand, symbolically marking the start of their newfound faith. A public profession of faith means that your faith may be personal, but it can't stay private. So making the invitation to faith was something I was resolutely ready and prepared to do.

But I was asked not to do it.

Instead the conference leaders asked me to set up the invitation without actually giving it. I had already addressed the believers in the room to give up the "one thing" keeping them from fully following Jesus. Students gave up everything from boyfriends to drug dealing so that Jesus could be their first love. Then I told those who hadn't yet followed Jesus that they would get an opportunity to receive God's forgiveness and fully surrender their lives to Jesus.

Then I dismissed them into their small groups.

For me, it was a weird moment. Every instinct shouted, "Make the invitation!" It felt almost disobedient to let it go.

But the conference leaders showed great wisdom. They had already trained the small group leaders to make an invitation to faith. When we broke up into small groups, the student leaders had their own opportunity to invite their friends to follow Jesus. If someone became a believer, they'd have instant community to help them along their new faith journey.

Of the thirty-one friends who hadn't yet followed Jesus before that weekend, twenty-seven of them surrendered their lives to trust Jesus fully.

In times long past, the Holy Spirit was only poured out on a few. The people of God would be fortunate if they had one person who heard the Lord in any given generation. In blessed times, there might have been a band of prophets, but the Spirit certainly wasn't poured out on everyone. It was just for a select few—the spiritual elite.

But sometime in the ninth century before the birth of Jesus, a promise was made that a time would come when the Spirit would no longer be restricted to a few. God's Spirit would no longer lurk behind a heavy, temple curtain nor be contained in a building.

Instead, the Spirit would be poured out on all people.

Young men would see visions.

Old men would see dreams.

Women and men, full of his Spirit, would prophesy in his name.

And the Spirit's presence would no longer be reserved just for the elite, but God would call everyone who has breath to praise his name and enjoy him forever. The Spirit would no longer dwell in a temple but find his home among the people of God.

Centuries later, this promise was fulfilled in Jerusalem when a band of believers was huddled in an upper room. They had already witnessed a miracle of miracles: their rabbi, Jesus, had come back to life! He told them to wait in Jerusalem until power came on them from on high.

Then it came: A rushing wind. Tongues of fire. The languages of the world, spoken. The Spirit broke out, and thousands were called to follow Jesus.

From that point on, the Spirit wasn't just for the educated, the elite, or the few. It was meant for all. All who call upon the name of Jesus have the gift of the Holy Spirit.

Yes, in all of us, he resides.

And also in each of us, he dwells.

God with us.

Immanuel.

Forever.

Yet for some reason, in the West, we sometimes fall back on a religion of the few, of the elite, of the educated. Seminaries must train, right? Surely, we need to have masters and doctoral degrees to lead? Only when we've mastered Greek, Hebrew, and show some level of exegetical prowess can we rightly preach, eh?

So we often keep church leadership to the few. Would we even let fishermen and tax collectors run our churches anymore? It's not that theological education isn't helpful, it is. It isn't the enemy. Yet the human inclination is to keep restricting leadership to just a few. Those who have been through the requisite training and education, only they can truly lead us. We fear the rest will somehow lead us astray, so we tend to professionalize everything. It gives people confidence to know that their leaders have the right educational and ecclesiastical credentials.

In the medieval church, the ability to read and interpret the Bible was reserved for the select few, so that even priests and monks were kept at a distance from the Bible. Martin Luther blew the lid off that paradigm by translating the Bible from Latin into the German tongue so that the common person could read and understand it.

Have we done with the Holy Spirit what the medieval church did with the Bible? Knowing our tendencies, perhaps God is showing us a different way. The Spirit won't be contained by our doctorates and diplomas.

The Spirit won't be poured out on just a few, but on the many.

The Spirit won't just be poured out on the educated but also on those who have had no formal education. The Spirit won't just be poured out on the elderly but also on the young. The Spirit won't just be poured out on men but also on women. The Spirit won't just be poured out on Jewish people, or Europeans, or Brazilians, Ghanians, Swedes, or Koreans only, but he is poured out on us all.

And this same Spirit gives to every single one of us a spiritual gift that can be used for the common good. All of us have a mission, because all of us have been gifted by the Giver of that mission.

Paul, in 1 Corinthians 12, goes even further. Not only do we each have a gift, but no one can opt-out of the Christian body. Paul put it this way: can the ear say to the eye that since I'm not an eye, I'm not a part of the body? No, of course not. And just because you don't have the gift of evangelism doesn't mean you don't have something to give. You're still called to be a witness, though you might do it differently than those who have gifts in evangelism who are supposed to equip others to share their faith. Just because you don't have healing gifts doesn't mean that you are left out. Those without gifts are still called to pray for the sick.

But more importantly, everyone has a gift; no one can be counted out.

In fact, those who seem to be in greater need should be even more honored. It's not about talent anymore, at least at a human level. It's not about what we're bringing to the table, really. It's about the fact that God has already given us a gift for the common good, and we all, in our own way, are called to offer something to the common good.

We are all on mission.

Everybody gets to play.

At the Azusa Street revival, the Spirit poured out on all people. Black or white, rich or poor, male or female, all who were there experienced the Spirit in a new and powerful way in that little alley in Los Angeles. They spoke in all manner of languages—some common, some heavenly—and a new movement would be born that would, just a century later, claim 279 million adherents. Add charismatic Christians as well, and that number balloons to 584 million.

At the revival prayer meetings, anyone could hear from God. The Spirit of God was the ultimate leveler: anyone could speak for God. At least, the community would take seriously what was said and discern together. That has a way of stripping away titles or status. Nothing else mattered. If you were in God's presence, and the community felt that someone spoke on behalf of God, that person had a spiritual authority bestowed upon them that others would follow.

Anyone could lead. Nothing was in the way because God's Spirit was in everyone.

It was like this in the early church. Rodney Stark, in *The Rise of Christianity*, highlights how the Christian faith grew from a marginal Jewish sect to become the dominant religion of the Roman Empire in four short centuries.

It's because everyone got to play.

People shared their faith with others, and through one-on-one relationships, rather than mass evangelistic events, the Roman Empire was converted. Women, not just men, were entrusted with leadership and given a higher level of status in the church than outside it. Rich and poor were gathered together, so that no one had need. During outbreaks of disease, the sick—both Christian and pagan—were cared for.

When everyone got to play, revival broke out. We can't do revivals alone.

Sure, there is the kind of quote that is often misattributed to John Wesley. When asked how he would attract such large crowds to his preaching, he reportedly replied, "I catch fire, and people come to watch me burn."

That can seem like an individual's story. But even in this quote, it's not just about Wesley. It's about the people he inspired and the folks they inspired. There was a cascading affect because everyone got to play.

Revivals may have someone spark them, but they never happen through just one person. Revivals, in their nature, must flow through relationships and communities. In the Methodist revival, John Wesley sought out his brother Charles Wesley. They formed the "Holy Club," a name given by other students, in mockery. They were too serious about their faith.

In order to burn hot, they had to gather the coals.

Everyone gets the chance to be a part of something significant. The most ordinary of us are capable of extraordinary things. Through our natural bodies, the supernatural can occur.

Everyone has a spiritual gift to offer the common good. No one is to be neglected or ostracized. Everyone has something to offer.

On Catalina Island, I could've invited people to follow Jesus from the front. I love doing it. And God might have had twenty-seven people stand to give their lives over to Jesus' leadership. I probably would've felt great about what God did, and enjoyed my part in it.

But instead, the opportunity was given to students. They were a mix of leaders, introverts and extroverts, cool and a little nerdy. But they were committed to the work to helping others find Jesus and fall in love with him. They all prayed beforehand and recruited others to pray with them, as well. Some of them had never asked someone to follow Jesus before, while others had never seen someone respond to Jesus' invitation to follow him.

Whether or not someone came to faith that weekend, they all got to play. Many of them got to be firsthand witnesses of the joy and faith that is released when twenty-seven people come to follow Jesus. And in that common experience, many of the leaders were hungry for more.

They did it together.

In revivals, everyone plays.

Scatter Widely

The parable of the sower is fascinating, in that the sower doesn't seem to be very good at what he does. He's not efficient. He doesn't seem to have a plan, a core process, or a sense of how to use the latest technology to get a bumper crop.

Indeed, the sower seems wasteful.

He just scatters the seed wildly, almost recklessly. It's prodigal. It's so generous that it seems foolish. It's just flung about, and whether it hits road or rocks, sand or soil, the seeds are just scattered far and wide.

Some will stick. Others won't.

It speaks of a God who gives everyone hundreds and thousands of chances. It's the kind of God who would create billions of uninhabited universes so that life could be found on one. It's the kind of God who would father billions of people in the hopes that all might fall back in love with him. He's a generous God, almost too generous, too patient, too giving, too wasteful.

But it also speaks of another truth: his resources are inexhaustible.

He just keeps giving.

In the same way, we want to be that generous with the teaching of the gospel—in word, deed, and power. We want to be generous with seeds of revival. We spread it around. We share our stories. We teach on it. We get the word out there.

As InterVarsity seeks revival for the next decade, we pray that every campus over 1,000 students would have an indigenous witnessing community—2,500 campuses in all. At the time of this writing, we're at 695.

It feels impossible.

In the early days when we were led by God toward this dream, it felt intoxicating. But what was once the stuff of heady dreams has become the seedlings of anxious nightmares. What were we thinking? How in the world are we going to get there? Even with the full-time equivalent of 1,400 campus ministers, we definitely don't have the earthly resources to accomplish this plan.

God will need to show up, and show up big.

We need revival.

Even if we combined the footprint of the eight largest campus ministries, we'd cover almost 1,200 campuses. With that, we'd have to still reach 1,300 campuses in partnership with other ministries to reach all of them in twelve years.

But as we've gotten the word out there, God is making some amazing connections for us with other communities that have the same heart for revival.

It's great to know we're not the only ones asking for it.

People all around the world have been spreading widely this idea of revival. For example, the International Fellowship of Evangelical Students, which serves a half million students worldwide, will host a conference called Revive Europe. Young people from forty European countries will come together, expectant for a move of God.

But hunger for revival isn't confined to campus ministries. We also hear about churches and church networks that seek revival as well. Some have made it their main focus. And we would love to see ways that campus ministries and church networks can work together so that everyone would get a chance to see, firsthand, a credible witnessing community and an opportunity to follow Jesus and be a part of his purposes in the world.

Get the word out. Let others know that you're seeking it. See who else comes along for the ride.

And as we spread our seeds widely, we notice that some will respond.

Discern Ripeness

Jesus tells another parable right after the last one. He's riffing on the same agricultural image, but now the farmer is paying attention to the crop that is growing. He's focused particularly on *how* it grows. Where there was a wastefulness in the spreading of seed, there is great care in the growing of the resulting stalk.

He doesn't control it; sleeping or awake, he really doesn't understand the full energy behind the seed and how it grows into sprout and stalk. Scientists can tell us how things go but not why. A life energy pulses through that seed, ready to burst forth under sun and shade.

But as it grows, first the stalk, then the head, then the grain, there's a progression. And the farmer is paying attention to how things are growing, because at some point, he needs to put the sickle to it—when it is ripe.

After we've scattered widely, we want to pay attention to how things are growing. We want to see how people are responding.

We're looking for future revival leaders.

As you pursue revival, people may come up to you, wanting to learn more, to pursue more, as if they're grabbing the hem of your garment and saying, "Let us go with you, because we have heard that God is with you." They've seen the fire in you and want to watch you burn.

When people are coming out of the woodwork, like sprouts out of soil, to come up to you, pay close attention.

We have a mutual friend and colleague, Serene, and she burns hot for Jesus. She has sworn off alcohol for years, as a consecrating activity, preparing herself for the work to come. She has a sense of calling about being a revival leader, particularly being the first of many female revival leaders in our movement. She has contended with Jesus, taking risk after risk to see God's kingdom move in word, deed, and power. She has taken many steps so that her character is more in line with the fruit of the Spirit, learning to reconcile, forgive, and to exhibit more patience in the name of the Lord.

Add that she's an incredibly gifted person, with an innovative and creative mind that is able to stretch the thinking of people around her. As much of a visionary that I might think I am, she makes me dream bigger, leading me to get closer to what God might have in store for us.

She teaches on the Holy Spirit throughout our movement, and after a weekend of speaking, she found herself wondering, *How should I measure success?* She didn't see the Spirit break out to the point where everyone was on the floor in tears, but she admitted that she was hoping for something big. She found herself at a loss.

She had one ray of hope, however. One student came up to her and shared that she wanted to be a revival leader too. She asked Serene to help her become one.

This is what Serene does. She already leads a network of female leaders who are seeking revival. She saw that there weren't many female revival leaders they could look up to as role models, so she gathered the coals together to burn hot. And as a woman who is multiracial—white and Chinese—she also has an eye for ethnic minority female leaders who could lead revival if it were to come.

Sometimes, when it comes to revivals, we want the bigger things, the things we can easily point to as the supernatural. We want God's Spirit to rush through like he did at Pentecost and really shake things up in a new and vibrant way. In looking for these kinds of things, Serene could have missed the greater miracle.

Someone was willing to follow her lead. And that's worth more than a momentary rush of wind, no matter how powerful.

Gather the Harvest

As we gather people, we don't just gather them to ourselves. We gather them to each other. We connect them with other people in Jesus' name.

Given technology today, my hope is that it will be easier to do this, not harder. What would it look like to gather people on the phone, online, over video, or by any means possible, so that revival leaders don't feel so alone?

There are so many people who are seeking God for the fullness of word, deed, and power yet don't know anyone in their immediate community who could help them. They are immediately ridiculed, considered too enthusiastic and a bit off-balance for seeking God too much. They need other like-minded, godly risk takers who are willing to do anything for Jesus, and in their company, to allow the fire to burn more steadily and faithfully.

We gather the coals to keep them hot, and scatter them so that others can burn. As the author of Hebrews encourages, "Let us consider how we may spur one another on toward love and good deeds, not giving up meeting together, as some are in the habit of doing, but encouraging one another—and all the more as you see the Day approaching."

It's in the rhythm of gathering and scattering that we have places for people to be encouraged to be hot, and then to be sent.

In our day, we need to find like-minded people to do life with. If we can jump into a local community or small group that is seeking revival, that is best. But if we can't find people like that, it could be easier to start with gathering potential revival leaders online, meeting by video, praying over the internet, and gathering them into virtual communities to keep up some semblance of encouragement and fire.

I (James) gathered a group of leaders who would seek revival together as a part of the National Council of Evangelists. We gathered together to pray and understand revival and to see how that could help people who didn't know Jesus get to know him. We met monthly for nine months, with two face-to-face meetings along the way. We had fun and were deeply encouraged. In the end, the fruit of that council is a heart for revival and a definition of revival that InterVarsity is in the process of taking on.

When we first started meeting, we had no idea the impact this group might have. Now, we see that it was one part out of many that is helping our movement to long for revival.

Send the Workers

Once we have a network like this, we need to give to it. It needs to be empowered and released. Why? Because there is still much harvest to gather. Jesus said, "The harvest is plentiful, but the workers are few." He even asked us to pray for more workers so they can be sent.

How does Jesus send out workers? In Luke 9:1-2, he sends them out with power and authority. Both are crucial.

The word *power* connotes the ability to do something. It's the resources to get things done. *Authority* is responsibility. Another way to put it is that it's the right to lead. If power gives you the resources needed, then authority gives you the right to lead. When Jesus sent out the disciples, the Scriptures make it clear that he gave them both power *and* authority. All of Jesus' resources and all of his rights have been given to you.

We have the right to enter any realm because we go in his name, which means in his authority. We're to make disciples of all nations, by going, baptizing, and teaching in the *name* of the Father, Son, and Holy Spirit. So we don't need permission to step into kingdoms of darkness and evil to bring the light. We have the right to be there, because the Creator of the universe has given us that right.

To help leaders thrive, we have to give them power and authority. They need both.

Offering power without authority leads to frustration. It's micromanagement. They have the gifts and resources to do the things we ask, but we keep making the decisions for them. If they don't have the final say, they aren't really in charge. This hamstrings rising leaders. Giving power without authority means that not everyone gets to play.

On the flip side, giving authority without power leads to burnout. It's overloading others who have the responsibility of making something happen but without the commensurate gifts or resources to do it. If they aren't resourced, they aren't thriving. It's like seeking revival without his Spirit. It grinds rising leaders. Giving authority without power means that people will give up playing.

To have an all-play culture, power and authority—both given by Jesus—are given and available to everyone who trusts in his name. They have already been granted to us. We don't do anything to earn them; they are received as gifts, graces to us, empowering us for kingdom work.

In revival leadership, power and authority are given to all. We equip others so that revivals can continue to thrive and grow. Ministry leader Steve Addison writes, "Movements spread ... through the efforts of ordinary people who inspire and equip key leaders."

Equip others and let everyone play.

The Moravians showed this kind of rhythm. They met together in Herrnhut to pray around the clock. In the farmland on the eastern edge of Germany, they found the coals gathered, and they would grow hot, praying in his name. They prayed round the clock. And through prayer, they found intimacy in Jesus, the kind that would later spark the Methodist movement as John Wesley found his heart strangely warmed.

But they also scattered. The first Protestant missionary force came from the Moravians, at first a community of three hundred, as they sent their people far and wide. Everyone got to play. They went out, two-by-two, one to primarily work to support the work of the other in their explicit missionary enterprises.

In their first thirty years, hundreds more were sent out. And the quality of these missionaries was evident, even to a younger John Wesley. When storms would lash their ships, they would exhibit tremendous peace while others were terrified.

And as they were sent, they each did their part to change the world.

Discussion Questions

1. To whom are you meant to scatter widely the seeds of revival?

2. Who are you meant to bring together to encourage them about revival?
3. How have you seen power but not authority given to leaders? How have you seen authority given to leaders but not power?
4. What are some ways to give power and authority to others so they can start to learn how to lead revival?

Chapter Nine

MYSTERY AND STRATEGY PARADOX

The intense religious experiences that give rise to new movements would remain fleeting unless embodied in some form of human organization.
STEVE ADDISON, *MOVEMENTS THAT CHANGE THE WORLD*

So after they had fasted and prayed, they placed their hands on them and sent them off.
LUKE TO THEOPHILUS, ACTS 13:3

Perhaps you know this feeling. Imagine that you've walked into the meeting room, and you see the smiling faces of your ministry partners. You can see the steam from their coffee mugs, rising like incense. They lead something with you, whether it's a pastoral staff team or just a couple others who help you lead the small group.

Whatever the team may be, someone opens the meeting with a prayer.

And from that point on, you catch up with ministry briefings. You might evaluate the last gathering, both its high points and its lows. You talk about particular people, about specific strategies. You come to some consensus about where you're going next. And then someone closes the meeting in a prayer.

There's a nice symmetry to it: your meetings were bookended with prayer. And yes, you were a part of a thoughtful discussion and came to a good decision. It's hard to deny that God's wisdom was really there.

But if you were honest with yourself, beside the topics of what you were talking about, it could've been a bunch of atheists gathered together to meet. Our prayers were spiritual, but the center of these meetings felt absent of a holy presence.

Is this how Christian ministry meetings are supposed to be? Is this how revival happens?

Perhaps you come from the other side of the spectrum. Imagine that you're all sitting on the floor of a dimly lit room stuffed with throw pillows and flickering candles. Someone in the corner is playing chords on a guitar. You offer prayers with your eyes shut, swaying rhythmically as branches in the wind of God's Spirit.

Much has been interceded for. Many words have been spoken about what God is saying or what he will do. And an honest encouragement rises in the room. It's hard to deny that God's presence was really there.

But after the last amen, it's hard to tell if anything is different. You had a great experience with like-minded souls, yet nothing really seemed to change. Emotions were stirred, your hearts were slightly warmed, and images and words were shared, but you don't have a sense of direction or purpose.

It all starts to feel, ironically, a little routine.

Over months, a subtle-but-sure jadedness has covered you, and you wonder if God is actually on the move at all.

Is this how we're supposed to feel? Is this how revival breaks out?

Both perspectives seem to miss something, but there's a way to blend the best of both worlds—to find something that will take the best of our minds and our souls, and help us move forward to lead in revival.

But to receive it, you'll have to embrace a paradox.

Nehemiah: Practical and Spiritual

One definition of paradox is "a seemingly absurd or self-contradictory statement or proposition that when investigated or explained may prove to be well founded or true."

In other words, a paradox is seemingly contradictory, but it might be true.

Like Jesus being fully human and fully divine. Like our salvation being fully God's choosing and fully our choice. And perhaps it's also true when it comes to both the practical and the overtly spiritual. Perhaps it's mystery *and* strategy.

In the Scriptures, Nehemiah stands out as a revival leader who seemed to hold this paradox together well. Early in the book of Nehemiah, we learn a few things about him. He's part of the Jewish remnant living in Babylon. He comes from a line of migrants who were forcibly taken from their land. And in this foreign land, under the thumb of their oppressors, Nehemiah finds himself in an esteemed position.

He was cupbearer to the king.

As cupbearer, he was a trusted hand of the king and thus important and influential. One obvious function was to bring the king his drink. Sounds easy, right? Nope.

Lots of people wanted the king dead. Thus, the food and drink of the king had to be free of poisons. So the job of the cupbearer: not only to fully stock the cellars with the best of wines so that a cup is always ready but also to keep the drink of the king safe.

If you couldn't trust the cupbearer, who could you trust?

Add that he would also bear the signet ring and be the chief financial officer. It's hard to get all of that from the title of cupbearer, but Nehemiah was doing fine by worldly standards.

When his brother Hanani returned from the homeland of Judah with some other men, they brought back news that the land was in "great trouble and disgrace." The walls were down, the gates, burned. It was a ruin, a reminder of their disobedience to their God. They had broken the covenant with him and, as a consequence, were now in disarray.

It's here that Nehemiah's response should be noted. First, he sat down and wept. He let his emotions fill him rather than fighting them. And for days he "mourned and fasted and prayed before the God of heaven." His first response was a consecrating response. It was to go to God in his sorrow and to pray. To seek guidance; to ask for forgiveness; to remind himself of God's promises.

To do that, he prayed "day and night."

Praying is rarely my first response. I (James) tend to go straight to strategy. What's the problem we're trying to fix? What are the causes behind it? What are the possible solutions? Which are the most effective for the least amount of cost? What are my next steps? I can go right into the planning of a strategic response.

But not Nehemiah. He prayed. He asked God for help. And gave himself over to the work of understanding what God might have to say. And he didn't just pray for a day but for four months, which would fuel his actions.

Which leads to the second point, which might not seem like the first: he planned.

When it came time, he had a strategic course of action—which the Bible recounts. The members of the court were expected to shine with joy as they served the king. Letting his face fall was a punishable offense, but he did it anyway. And his timing wasn't random either. The queen wasn't always present in the king's court, but she was present on the day Nehemiah made his ask. Perhaps it was another way to tilt the odds in his favor, so that the king might show him mercy.

All of this is an intentional, if indirect, conversation starter. It was strategic, if not also risky.

The king wasn't slow, and picked up on it. He responds: "Why does your face look so sad when you are not ill? This can be nothing but sadness of heart."

Nehemiah doesn't spoil this opportunity and is already prepared with what he's going to say. He tells him the reason, that his home city lies in ruins.

The king, understanding what was happening, asked the blunt question. "What do you want?"

Nehemiah's list is ready. He asked to be sent to the city, with diplomatic letters for safe passage, with a letter—a blank check, of sorts—to the keeper of the royal park so that he can have timber to build the city's gates and temple. Since all of this would have to be transported along treacherous, bandit-ridden roads, Nehemiah knew that a security detail would be implied. When he left, the king also sent an armed caravan, complete with army officers and cavalry, to escort him on the long journey back to Israel.

As the book of Nehemiah unfolds, it's easy to see the ticktock of prayer and planning, asking God and inspecting the walls at night, seeking his face while casting vision, fasting while delegating the construction near family homes for maximum motivation, asking God to remember while he avoids being lured into a profane trap.

In this narrative, prayer and planning don't seem separate from each other. Ticktock wouldn't really be the right way to explain it, actually. It's more cohesive than that.

The prayer and planning energize each other: mystery and strategy.

And it's by holding both of these values together that we set ourselves up for revival leadership. The mystery is the wind, yet strategy allows us to hoist the sail that would catch as much of the wind as possible.

Mystery and Strategy Paradox

Sometimes, mystery and strategy are presented as polar opposites along a single spectrum. If you're a flaming charismatic, you're at one end of the mystery side. You'd rather worship at

Jesus' feet, pray with fervor, and pour out your emotions to seek his divine intervention at every turn or transition of the day.

If you're a disciplined activist, you might land squarely on the strategy edge. You've been blessed with a quick mind and a keen sense for true north. You've read the latest books on change management or leadership development—religious and secular—and you know your stuff.

Sometimes, these types are set in opposition.

But what if they weren't enemies squaring off but actually two different aspects of how we lead others? Instead of being on a linear scale, what if it was actually more of a two-dimensional grid?

On this four-quadrant graph, the horizontal axis represents strategy, while the vertical axis represents mystery. If you're closer to the left or the bottom, that's "low." When closer to the top or the right, that's "high."

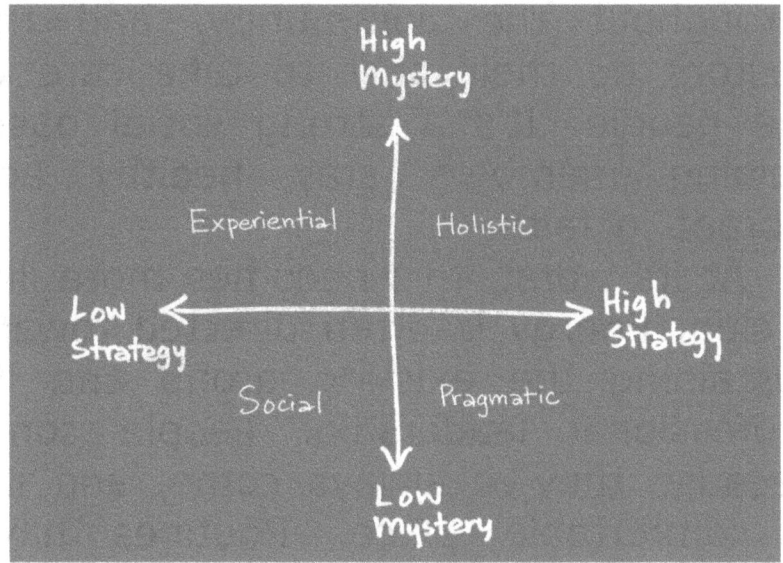

Figure 6. Strategy and mystery grid

Where on this graph would you place your community? Where would you place yourself?

The Social Quadrant: Low-Mystery/Low-Strategy

Some would fall in the low-mystery/low-strategy category. That doesn't mean that everything is bad.

Many churches fall into this category. At its best, it has elements of a strong community. People meet in small groups. Scriptures are studied and taught. Discipleship happens at some level of vibrancy. Prayer happens throughout the community, and the pastors do their best to take care of the people. It's a strong social base, helping members stay healthy and vibrant in faith.

At its worst, this becomes more like a club. Energy is often directed toward sustaining the existing group and its professional leadership. People come because they've always come, and it's a comfortable place. Routines have ossified; apathy has set in. It's about keeping the lights on when the soul has gone dark.

Either way, it's low on the mystery side because the community doesn't rely much on the Holy Spirit.

Using the word-deed-power paradigm, the power circle would be a pinhole in this quadrant. People don't pray for healing. The community may even have theology that says miracles don't happen or a history of bad experiences with what others called the "move of the Spirit."

No expectancy exists.

It's also low on the strategy side, because there isn't any intentionality in reaching out to others in their neighborhoods or workplaces either. They don't think about intentional steps to help their people grow to be missionaries in their schools or civic groups. No one is developing them to become leaders who can influence the world around them. Most of the energy is going into maintaining current programming, like Sunday services and other service projects.

Evangelism barely registers. The missional energy has dwindled.

When a community is low in both mystery and strategy, it is usually inward facing. Most of its resources tend to flow inward rather than outward.

In that way, churches and communities like these can actually last a long time, particularly if the pastors are great at caring for their congregation. Others are ready to close or be folded into another congregation. Some still have enough resources to get by, day-by-day, but you get the sense that things have dug into a routine.

When I (Ryan) first became a campus minister with Inter-Varsity, the fellowship I served had a strong value for community and discipleship. Once,

I interviewed every graduating senior in the ministry and found that the community was the top reason they loved being a part of the fellowship.

But they hated evangelism.

As is often said, "Culture eats strategy for breakfast." When I tried to gather all the small group leaders around an idea to begin leading non-Christian friends in short, accessible Bible studies we called GIGs—Groups Investigating God—they unanimously rejected the idea. They complained that it would water down our commitment to God's Word and turn us into a seeker-friendly group. We don't go wide, we go deep.

When I tried to disciple a freshman in evangelism that same year, he pushed back hard: "If I wanted to grow in evangelism, I would have joined Campus Crusade. I want to be discipled."

This fellowship rightly valued community and Scripture, but they didn't have any missional strategies to help people get to know Jesus or to experience God more deeply in prayer or mystery.

If you find yourself or your community in the social quadrant, gather some people in your community and begin a rhythm of gathering for prayer as a first step. Start asking, If revival were to come to our community, what would it look like? Then pray that God would offer or confirm a specific calling to revival. What is your particular mission for this season? Be open to what he might say to you. If he does offer something specific, then begin to pray—and potentially plan—for that as well.

The Experiential Quadrant: High-Mystery/Low-Strategy

Other communities are high in mystery but low in strategy. They're open to the move of the Holy Spirit. It can be a church with charismatic or Pentecostal leanings, or they can be smaller communities in churches, homes, or storefronts.

Expectation runs high in these circles: they don't limit God. He can do anything. They've witnessed miraculous healings in their midst and often hear words directly from God. They heard stories where God has answered in power. Worship is intense and powerful.

But when it comes to reaching those around them, they have little direction or purpose. Intentionality, at least in planning, isn't their strong suit. They tend to wait on God's leadership, praying together in huddles, waiting for God to speak. And once in a while, one of them is sent to mission, whether it's overseas or next door. It's a leading from the Holy Spirit, which isn't to be underestimated, yet they're often sent without training or development.

They have enough bright spots where they can point to God moving. They've sent a missionary to China, and she's already been used to heal two people in a village. They pray for her. Many are coming to faith through her actions. And truly, the mission is moving.

But they don't have a strategy around it, so it never grows. It's even tougher to sustain. It doesn't move beyond that missionary. She calls people to pray, but there isn't a sense of how this work will continue forward. Her influence is limited to that village.

At other times, they have sent others out, and nothing has happened. They went to the mall, and in their conversations, no one has joined their community. Others have failed, and they try again, and when nothing happens, there is no debrief, no learning. It's just given over to God's will, more of an inshallah kind of mentality. They can be fatalistic about their results. They shrug their shoulders and ask God to move again.

We call these kinds of communities *experiential.* To their credit, they are open to the move of God, which is a huge move forward. But without strategy, good ideas may not have the structures needed to sustain the word God has breathed into them. With this flash-in-the-pan effect, the ministry fails to grow and help more and more people get to know Jesus. Or, when it does fail, they don't learn from the failures and mistakes, in effect shutting down their God-given intellect, and allow themselves to be like grist for the mill in the name of God's will.

In a sermon, Tim Keller recounted how he was part of a revival during his college years at Bucknell University. A couple of students in the InterVarsity chapter there had "an amazing experience of the Spirit of God," and started to ask God for a vision for reaching the campus. Soon afterward, they saw their fledgling group bloom from fifteen students to 150 in a year. Half of the growth was new Christians, even without an organized approach.

The fellowship was organic. They were spontaneous. They didn't have officers or committees. They didn't have any plans. But the Spirit of God was deeply present in their gatherings, so much so that Keller himself became a Christian through this revival.

But as it progressed, students began to overemphasize the spontaneous over organization. "God never blesses planning," they cried.

They couldn't pass leadership on to anyone. They couldn't train people in what they had learned. Heresies crept into the group. It was missing "the backbone of organization."

Three years later, it was gone.

If you find yourself or your community in the experiential quadrant, then you could afford to lean toward strategies. As a first step, ask yourself, If revival were to move in our community, what would need to be in place to sustain it? Who would offer leadership to see this through? How would you organize gatherings so that people could take their next steps toward this calling? If God is leading, what longer-term vision would your community be open to committing to? If you start to plan around these ideas, you may begin to sustain some of the work of the Spirit that's flowing through you.

The Pragmatic Quadrant: Low-Mystery/High-Strategy

Some communities are low in mystery but high in strategy. These communities, typically, don't rely much on the power of God's Spirit as well, but they do their best to make up for it with strategy.

They have it in spades. The leadership reads the latest business books and leadership journals, scouring them for the next great idea. They go to lots of conferences and look for new ways to organize their Sunday programming, or their cell groups, or their parking volunteers. Leaders who can get results have great credibility in this quadrant.

These communities see growth. For some, it's quite a lot. They've studied their users, understood their motivations, and created ways to meet their needs. These leaders are savvy to cultural trends and have lush music and skilled orators who can connect with people's needs.

They're pragmatic.

Again, none of these things are wrong on their own, and these kinds of communities really have influence. They have the numbers, the finances, the page views, the likes, the downloads, the headlines, and thus, the cultural power to move things forward. Their pastors are interviewed in magazines and on network television, and many are doing numerically and financially well. They've got buildings, bucks, and butts.

But they can get exhausted. They, sometimes unconsciously, believe that the results they are getting are because of their effort. Leaders in these kinds of communities are often in counseling for stress and anxiety. They put the world on their shoulders and feel like it's on them to make the ministry grow. Burnout is common.

Most notable, however, is that their sense of wonder is absent.

They are going through the motions, editing the video announcement, debriefing the Sunday talks, and yet wonder if God is present. They have ceased to be amazed.

We put these kinds of churches and communities in the pragmatic quadrant. And although, like the experiential communities, much true and real good can come out of them, pragmatic communities can also create a sense of weariness. It ceases to feel like the "unforced rhythms of grace" that Jesus promised.

When we can point to our efforts and strategies as the main reason something grows, then a sense of awe and wonder becomes numb. It's not as easy to give God credit, much less glory. We see it as the work of our own hands, and the work of skilled and savvy marketers, to grow the might and influence of this ministry.

Many megachurches and movements could land here. Again, we're not faulting them. Many, if not most, of them have great leaders, great staff, great volunteers, great processes. They're often relevant and effective.

But is there a reliance on God's Spirit for the work that we see? When people drop by in the middle of the week to see the work, can they tell the difference between what happens there and what happens in the corporate or secular nonprofit world?

If God's people are living temples of the living God, shouldn't something feel different?

I (James) was recently at the Urbana Student Missions Conference. St. Louis wasn't as cold as it usually has been at that time of year, as over ten thousand delegates packed the Edward Jones Dome to meet God and learn how to be a "faithful witness" in the world.

I went to a local grocery store with an excellent selection for lunch. For me, it's the California Melt: a turkey and cheese panini with bread soaked and toasted in butter. Delicious.

But what made it even better was running into an old colleague, Mark, who was also hosting Robel, the general secretary of the Ethiopian International Fellowship of Evangelical Students (IFES) movement called EvaSUE. I've always wanted to meet him; the ministry he leads is on every campus in Ethiopia and fifty thousand students strong—with only seventy campus ministers!

They dwarfed the American IFES movement—InterVarsity USA—with a fraction of our staff.

I wanted to set up a meeting with Robel, to learn more from his leadership and their movement. But he humbly said, almost waving his hands to say that meeting up wasn't necessary, "All we do is give the ministry to students." I had the nagging feeling, however, that what he meant by that, and what we mean by that, were chasms apart.

I invited both him and Mark to an IFES roundtable discussion happening at the same conference, where Western campus movements could learn from the global majority. And for an hour, around twenty-five leaders from all over the globe discussed our strategies. As the discussion went on, I kept thinking that we've tried some of these things before, but they haven't taken off the way they do in Ethiopia or other parts of the world.

But near the end of the meeting, Mark made a striking comment. He said, as an American, what struck him in his visits to Ethiopia was their spiritual fervor. When they have a six-day student leadership conference, the entirety of one of those days would be spent in fasting and prayer. They trusted that God would move powerfully and that strategies alone wouldn't suffice.

Spiritually, they were white-hot.

I couldn't help but think that if we did that in our movement—a day dedicated to fasting and prayer—we'd have a revolt.

If you or your community falls in the strategic quadrant, consider adding more time in your meetings to pray as a first step. Set aside a quarter of your time to pray. If you have an hour meeting, spend fifteen minutes in prayer. If two hours, then spend a half hour. It's not that the length of time itself is the major emphasis, but it does press you into a deeper rhythm of prayer. Some of that prayer could be used to confess the ways we've relied solely on strategies—and renounce them so you can be more open to God's Spirit.

It's surprising how hard it is to start the rhythm of praying that long in meetings. It's not as surprising to share how difficult it is to keep that kind of rhythm going.

As you pray, listen. Hear what God might have to say. What if, in a ninety-minute strategy session, you took the last ten minutes to debrief and listen to God in prayer? Or what if you took periodic breaks during the meeting to take time to hear what God might have to say? Perhaps someone might discern something from Scripture, or perhaps someone in your community feels comfortable sharing something else. In it all, the others should weigh carefully what is said.

The Holistic Quadrant: High-Mystery/High-Strategy

Of course, when it comes to four-quadrant grids like figure 6, the quadrant that remains is the ideal one, right? Cynicism aside, it seems that revival could flow best out of these kinds of communities.

On one hand, it's the kind of leadership or community that is deeply open to God's Spirit moving. Bending a Josh McDowell quote, it's open to God's Spirit, but not so open that our brains fall out.

We're thankful that, for the most part, the debates of the '80s and '90s around the spiritual gifts seem to have quieted down. Many communities that were once, either by doctrine or just by lack of practice, not open to the move of God's Spirit, now see the necessity of God's wonder-working power to fuel and energize their faith communities. In many places, we've seen a greater openness to healings, prophetic words, and deliverance.

Given the darkness, depression, strife, and madness of our day, how could we go forward in hope if God were not with us, moving in powerful ways? I wonder if that's a reason why the Pentecostal movement, though just barely a century old, is one of the largest and fastest-growing denomination groups in the world.

At the same time, in holistic communities this openness to God's Spirit doesn't take away from compelling strategies. In these communities, there are intimate connections to God in faith, but it's not emotionalism. They're not centered on creating emotive experiences. Holistic communities allow people to interact with the living God, then move forward in thoughtful, creative, and strategic ways. They don't point to the gifts themselves but to the Giver. They can see healings and deliverances in their midst but humbly highlight God's power and not the particular person he is working through.

Many faith communities often reach this quadrant by way of another one.

They may more naturally land in either the social, experiential, or pragmatic quadrant but may make efforts to move toward being holistic. Some communities get there for a season. Under stress, however, they may fall back to the quadrant they came from. For example, a pragmatic community begins to be open to the Holy Spirit in new ways. But after a while, if they don't reach their goals, they may be tempted to slide back into the pragmatic quadrant and double down on analysis and strategy.

Holistic communities take the time to hear from God and try things out at his leading, but then they come back and debrief what just occurred. They learn from their joys and mistakes. They have raised the sail: it doesn't power the boat on its own, but their strategies are ways to catch as much of the wind that the Spirit might decide to blow as possible.

In one stark entry in Wesley's journal, he wrote about a time in Pembrokeshire, England, where a great revival had broken out in response to his preaching and evangelism. But when he returned twenty years later, no evidence of their evangelistic success remained. He concluded:

> I was more convinced than ever that the preaching like an apostle, without joining together those that are awakened and training them up in the ways of God, is only begetting children for the murderer. How much preaching has there been for these twenty years all over Pembrokeshire! But no regular societies, no discipline, no order or connection. And the consequence is that nine in ten of those once awakened are now faster asleep than ever.

He vowed never again to preach in an area that didn't have a ministry structure to sustain what God had done. He'd commit himself to planting classes and bands ahead of time, so that when revival came, they would be able to see it through to its fullest.

Many revivals fizzle out without strategy and organization, as Wesley observed. Steve Addison wrote on the same idea:

The intense religious experiences that give rise to new movements would remain fleeting unless embodied in some form of human organization. This presents every new movement with a dilemma—how to keep from extinguishing the "charismatic moment" that generates white-hot faith (the first key to a movement's vitality) while giving it sustained expression in social forms. When a movement fails to define itself in organizational forms, we are left with "a loose, ill-defined set of practices and ideas spreading within a population that is never weaned off its traditional commitments." This is a fad, not a movement.

Although revivals have ebb and flow, they shouldn't be a fad. They need form and structure.

When Ryan came on as a campus minister at UCSD, the chapter was in the social quadrant of figure 6. If they'd wanted to do evangelism, they would've gone elsewhere. But under his leadership, they started to move toward the pragmatic quadrant, finding evangelistic strategies that would work with college students. People became believers. When I arrived on campus, I introduced listening prayer through "daily" prayer meetings (which were really only four times a week), and also started teaching on spiritual gifts. We started to see prayer and healing in our ministry. Later, Ryan would pour spiritual fire on the wood by calling the campus ministers to fast often. At the ministry's height, we were operating in the holistic quadrant.

How can our communities be more holistic, seeking both mystery and strategy?

It's a tension we continue to fine-tune so that revival can come.

Discussion Questions

1. Of the four quadrants in figure 6, where would your faith community fit? Why?
2. What are one or two strategic ways that your community could move to the holistic quadrant?
3. When you pray, what does God say to you about how your

community could move to the holistic quadrant?

Chapter Ten

COMMUNAL DISCERNMENT

To manipulate, drive or manage people is not the same thing as to lead them.
DALLAS WILLARD, *HEARING GOD*

We do not know what to do, but our eyes are on you.
JEHOSHAPHAT OF JUDAH, 2 CHRONICLES 20:12

I (James) wanted to stay in Boston. I had lived there for eleven years, and it was a spiritual home for me. It was where my faith had been restored, and I saw God move powerfully in mission.

But when my wife was accepted into a top-five political science doctoral program in San Diego, we knew we were heading out west.

When we arrived, I joined the UCSD InterVarsity campus ministry team. Since I had six years of team leader experience from my time in Boston, they added me as a second team leader.

And this is where history becomes important.

The InterVarsity ministry at UCSD was divided into two chapters: North and South. Combined, they regularly had 150 students coming to large groups, although their reach was larger than that. Five years earlier, they had been one chapter of about 300, but given classroom sizes, it was hard to see how the chapter would grow. So the idea was to divide into two—North and South—based on geography.

UCSD has six colleges. Each college has its own flavor: imagine Hogwarts, but in the coastal hills of La Jolla. At the time I arrived in 2002, North served Marshall and Roosevelt, while South served Revelle, Muir, Warren, and Sixth.

After splitting, the InterVarsity chapters formed their own cultures. Students, of course, didn't stay within the designated geographic boundaries; they went to the chapter that suited them.

North was more evangelistic and often had irreligious people as a part of its fellowship. But it needed more discipleship, as some of the leaders were known to get drunk on weekends. South was nerdier yet more spiritually devoted. They had fewer people who didn't know Jesus, but they prided themselves in the ways they dove deep into Scriptures and sought to live out their faith.

Needless to say, the fellowships didn't like each other much.

There used to be two campus ministry teams that oversaw the fellowships: one for North and one for South. But the year before I got there, they reorganized. Instead of dividing the ministry teams by geography, they divided by function. So the evangelism team was born, and they started the freshmen ministry for both chapters as well as a campus-wide evangelistic event called the Edge. Ryan was the leader of this team, and he hand-picked some campus ministers and some freshmen, and they were given permission to lead out in evangelism. They started to see people come to faith in droves.

Still, the move was done without the consent of South chapter leaders, and tension between the ministry team and the students was at an all-time high.

Add the other ministry team into the picture. They were dubbed the Training team—boring!—and it was hard for them not to feel like leftovers. I, the outsider, was tapped to lead them. We led the crews in charge of large groups (our all-community weekly gatherings), small groups, and other programming, but since I had a heart for evangelism, we started doing things like public invitations to faith in large groups.

Both teams covered both chapters in their different spheres, and it was getting messy. As you can also imagine, there were tensions between these two ministry teams, often rooted in envy, jealously, or a lack of single-minded vision.

Ryan and I were at an area team meeting where both of our teams were present, and in a side conversation, he wondered if North and South chapters should merge. And that thought lodged in my head. I couldn't shake it. So I started praying and planning to see if we could move in that direction.

Then we brought it up to the seventy student leaders. At the time, most of the leaders from both chapters were dead set against it. We were stuck.

How do we discern God's leading in a situation like this?

The Discipleship Cycle

When leading revival, we obviously need to be open to God's leading. But much of what we do in Christian leadership is to meet to find discernment as we discuss and strategize. I wonder if there's another way for Christian communities to create spaces for God to speak to our entire community to help us move forward in his mission.

If a community hears the Lord together, it has a way of energizing purpose and direction that can only be envied by our best leaders. But what are the practical steps in leading communal discernment of God's leadership?

In InterVarsity, we have a tool called the Discipleship Cycle that we've found helpful in communal discernment.

The Scriptures offer us various models of how communal discernment could happen, but one that stands out to me occurred under Jehoshaphat's reign in Judah. In 2 Chronicles 20, Jehoshaphat hears about a three-nation alliance marching toward Judah from the southeast. The Moabites, Ammonites, and Meunites had come to wage war against Judah with a vast army. Judah was outnumbered.

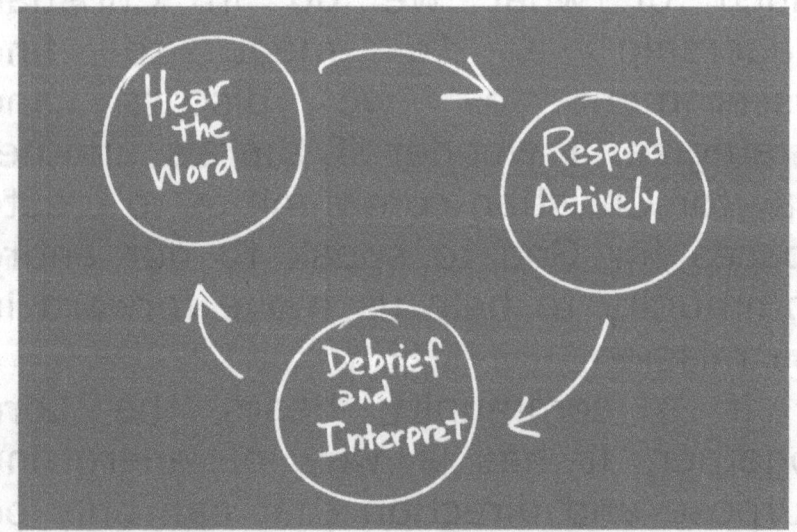

Figure 7. The discipleship cycle

If you were leading this nation, what would you do? What would normal leaders do? Wouldn't it be wise to get the generals and start preparing for a hefty defense? Do our scouts know anything more about the swarm of people coming toward us? How are they armed? What kind of weaponry do they have? And what kind of defenses do we have? What is the state of our walls? How many men do we have to fight this army? Where are potential weak spots that our enemy can exploit?

But Jehoshaphat has a different response. He wasn't full of courage out of the gate. The text tells us that he was "alarmed." And in that state, he immediately called a nationwide fast. All the people gathered to him in Jerusalem to pray before God.

When they came together, Jehoshaphat prayed in front of the temple. He prayed about the might of their God and the history of his mighty power in the past. And he also confessed, in front of the entire people that he was called to lead, that "We do not know what to do, but our eyes are on you."

It's a disarmingly vulnerable prayer. The situation was completely overwhelming and the nation's survival and livelihood were at stake, yet the king fully admitted he didn't have the foggiest idea of how they might take on this threat.

Can you imagine the president of the United States getting up in front of teleprompter to say that Russia, China, and Iran have joined forces to attack us, so let's get together to pray on the Washington Mall because he has no idea what to do? He'd be impeached. (Or these days, maybe not.)

Yet they stand there, all of Judah. All the men, their "wives and children and little ones" stood before God.

A sword couldn't cut that silence.

Hear the Word

At this point, I want to stop the story to highlight the first step in communal discernment. Jehoshaphat is an amazing revival leader because his first instinct is to call the community together to pray—and to listen to what God might have to say.

It's that initial instinct that sets apart revival leaders.

In response, the Spirit of the Lord fell on Jahaziel—who was of the priestly clan and likely a songwriter—and he replies to the king. He received a message, and he told the king and everyone else not to be afraid. God would win this battle. The army was climbing up by the Pass of Ziz, and the people only needed to march down against them at the end of the gorge in the Desert of Jeruel.

They wouldn't need to fight, just prepare and take up positions.

Then they would see what God would do.

How can we create spaces for God to speak to us in real life situations? Scripture study and prayer meetings really are the first things that come to mind. Come together around the study of Scripture, and allow people to share what they're seeing God say through his Word. Or come together in prayer, and try to hear what God might have to say.

In this passage, after hearing such a courageous word, the people have to discern whether it's from God or not. It's here that Jehoshaphat becomes a revival leader. He sensed that the word was from God. He then falls with his face to the ground and the entire nation follows him in worship of God. Then the priests—worship leaders!—praised the Lord with a loud voice.

They knew they had a word from God. But how do we know?

In *Real Life,* I (James) wrote that the key skill every follower of Jesus should seek is to recognize God's voice and obey what he says.

When leading revival, we don't just need to hear God for ourselves. How can we create communal spaces for others to recognize God's voice and obey what they hear together? For in my experience, when it comes to motivating a community, one word from God is worth a thousand sermons.

Ultimately, we learn to discern by familiarity. The more you get to know God, the more you'll recognize what he is trying to say to you. But to be helpful, I'll also break that down into five questions of discernment. They should help you understand more readily what God might be saying.

Is it biblical? In Acts 17:11, the Berean Jews were considered of more noble character than the Thessalonians—poor Thessalonians!—because they both received the message with great eagerness yet tested everything that Paul and Barnabas said against the Scriptures. They had an openness to the new word yet went back to the Scriptures to see if it lined up with the revelation they already knew. And when testing an idea or thought that someone claims is from the Lord, it is good to test that claim against what has already been revealed in the Scriptures.

What did you hear in prayer? In John 10:4, Jesus said that the sheep will know the voice of the shepherd. He's pulling from an Ancient Near Eastern image where different flocks of sheep were often kept in a common pen at night so that shepherds could take turns at the night watch. When the morning came and the shepherd needed to take his flock to pasture, he would call out, and the sheep would self-sort, recognizing the voice of their own shepherd. Jesus seems to be saying that we, too, will be able to recognize God's voice in the cacophony of others that try to drown him out. With that promise, it seems that we should also pray for discernment. When people come up to me for guidance about what they should do with their lives, I'll respond by asking, When you prayed about it with others, what did you hear? And often, they'll sheepishly look at their shoes and say that they haven't prayed with anyone about it.

What if fear wasn't involved? In the letter 1 John, the phrase "God is love" is repeated so often that the two are seen as equals. So when John writes in 4:18 that "Perfect love drives out fear," it seems that in God, fears can be cast out. Of course, there is still awe and wonder of God—a fear that is out of respect—but the debilitating, paralyzing fear can cease. So this may be my favorite question of the five: What would you do if fear was not involved? If you weren't afraid, what would you do? I think you would get closer to what God might be saying to you.

Does it produce the fruit of the Spirit? In Galatians 5:22-23, the fruit of the Spirit is described as "love, joy, peace, forbearance, kindness, goodness, faithfulness, gentleness and self-control." It's basically a list of nine markers that show you if you're becoming more like Jesus, or not. Is a word from God bringing more of this fruit in our lives, or is it bringing the opposite? If someone claims to bring a word from God, but we find them exhibiting the opposite fruit, such as hate, despair, anxiety, impatience, meanness, selfishness, mistrust, aggression, and self-indulgence—then even if they are saying something that resembles truth, they are not saying it in God's Spirit. So it doesn't need to be accepted. It could be tested, and possibly resisted, by this standard.

What does the Christian community say about it? In 1 Corinthians 14:29, Paul gives this advice about prophetic words: that two or three should speak, and the others should test what they've said. Discerning God's voice was meant to be a communal affair. Sure, in the Old Testament, it was more solitary. But back then, the Spirit of God was sent on a few in a given generation, sometimes only one. That's why Israel had to stone prophets when they were wrong. As Jordan Seng put it in *Miracle Work,* they had to exercise "tight editorial control." But when the prophecy in Joel was fulfilled in Acts 2, the Spirit is poured out on all believers young and old, women and men. In that way, it became safer to speak on behalf of God, because the locus of discernment was no longer in one person but dispersed throughout the community. We were meant to discern the will of God together, so why do we try to discern God's will on our own?

If you can answer all five questions in the affirmative, then you are closer to discerning God's voice or will.

In Jehoshaphat's case, the five questions were answered in the affirmative.

Is it biblical? Yes, the word aligned with what they knew in the Scriptures. Israel was still under God's covenant, and if they were faithful, God would bring blessing and protection upon their land. What the prophets spoke came out of a time of prayer. And the answer they were given would make them still face their fears more than escape them, thus requiring less fear and more faith. As for fruit, it made them more joyful to hear that word collectively. And lastly, they did hear the word in community, and it was confirmed by the community as well.

Now, it doesn't mean that everything that passes these five questions is from the Lord, but my hope is that it will help you get closer to what God might be saying as you discern together in community.

Respond Actively

As the story progresses, Jehoshaphat is faced with a choice. They had heard the word of God the day before, and they were elated at the response. The community felt God's presence, and worship abounded. But by verse 20, it was early in the morning in the Desert of Tekoa. The dew might've been fresh on the ground, the smell of dampness wafting up in their noses. The army of Judah was there in full force, having put on their armor, riding their horses, banners lifted high. The sounds of many boots hitting the ground could be heard throughout the camp, and perhaps their nerves were on edge.

What they heard yesterday would be put to the test today.

But Jehoshaphat was sure. Watching what was happening around him, he offered up a word of encouragement to his troops. As author Philip Yancey once quoted: "Don't forget in the darkness what you have learned in the light." He may have heard the Lord again, as he shared something in the couplet rhythm of the prophets of old: "Listen to me, Judah and people of Jerusalem! Have faith in the Lord your God and you will be upheld; have faith in his prophets and you will be successful."

Then, to back it up, Jehoshaphat appoints worship leaders. They sing, and praise God. And they would be at the front of the army. It's like sending out U2 on the front lines, the Edge's guitar in hand, blaring away as they go to face this vast multitude.

It's foolish, isn't it?

Jehoshaphat led them into an active response. A word from God always demands response. Words from God never lead to passivity but draw us up in faith toward some sort of action. It could be argued that all Christian leadership is really just listening for God's direction and responding.

Jesus says the same thing in Matthew 7. He was at the end of probably the most famous sermon in all of history, and at the end of three chapters of instruction, he said this in conclusion:

> Everyone who hears these words of mine and puts them into practice is like a wise man who built his house on the rock. The rain came down, the streams rose, and the winds blew and beat against that house; yet it did not fall, because it had its foundation on the rock. But everyone who hears these words of mine and does not put them into practice is like a foolish man who built his house on sand. The rain came down, the streams rose, and the winds blew and beat against that house, and it fell with a great crash.

The difference between the wise man and the foolish man is not in the quality of the word they received. They both heard the truth. They both heard from Jesus.

The foolish man listens, and then does nothing about it. The wise man hears the words, and puts them into practice. Firm foundations are built not just by hearing, but in doing.

Thriving discipleship requires that if we hear a truth from God, we need to put it into practice as soon as we're able. This is the only way to build the foundations of our spiritual life. If we merely hear the word, and do nothing, no matter how stunning, insightful, or powerful the word was, it means nothing.

Our houses will come down with a crash.

After we lead times of communal discernment, if there is a sense that God said something to the community, you must act. Respond. Test it by doing something. That's how you grow as a spiritual leader and a disciple of Jesus.

Debrief and Interpret

Even though we take an action, however, it doesn't mean that all will go well.

In my twenties, if I heard a word from God, then I thought that my life would be all green lights. All the doors would open. I would be fully blessed as I followed that word.

But now, in my forties, if I hear a word of the Lord clearly, I start to wonder: *Why did God think I needed to hear it so clearly?*

It's likely because it's going to get harder before it gets better.

Even Jesus seems to say that. Even if we get it right—hearing the voice of the Lord correctly—it may still lead to persecution. In John 15:20, Jesus reminds us that if they persecuted him, they will persecute us also.

You can hear rightly and still suffer.

That's why it's important to debrief and interpret. It's best done in community. Some of us are good at hearing the word. Others are good at responding actively. Others are good at debriefing and interpreting. And we need all the parts of the body working together to help each other move along in constructive ways.

We need people to help us discern whether we responded rightly, wrongly, or somewhere in between, and then also to help us interpret how things went down. Perhaps we heard rightly to share our faith with our unbelieving parents, even though they rejected Jesus this time. Or perhaps we heard rightly, but we ended up shaming our parents in a way God hadn't asked us to.

We need mature people of faith to help us debrief and interpret.

Once we do that, we put ourselves at the feet of Jesus—through prayer and Scripture study—to hear what God might be saying to us today. And in this way, we are helping each other to be able to recognize God's voice in the everyday and to obey what we hear.

And if we help our communities do the same, won't we set ourselves up for revival? Shouldn't Christian leadership help us all hear God's voice more clearly and encourage us to respond?

We could end every gathering by asking, "What is God saying to you? And what are you going to do about it?" Isn't this precisely the kind of rhythm that would prepare us for revival?

The English village of Drayton-in-the-Clay (now Fenny Drayton) is home to one of the oldest circles of giant yew trees in the United Kingdom. In 1624, it's also the fitting place where George Fox was born.

Fox grew up as the son of a weaver in a well-to-do, yet strongly Puritan family. As a youth, he had a spiritual hunger. Beginning in 1643, he wandered throughout the country from one clergy member to another looking for answers. Still, he continued to intensely pray, fast, and study the Scriptures along the way.

In 1647, after he had given up on priests and preachers to show the way, he heard a voice: "There is one, even Christ Jesus, that can speak to thy condition." And when he heard it, his heart leapt for joy. This spiritual revelation gave him the conviction that Christ could speak to anyone—Jew or

Greek, male or female, slave or free. And if God spoke to everyone, then everyone was equally valuable in his sight.

Starting in 1652, Fox began to travel about and gather small groups of followers who would later become the movement known as the Society of Friends, more popularly known as the Quakers. They eschewed clergy and formalized religion, so in their meetings they would sit still in a circle, sometimes for hours, waiting for God to speak through someone—anyone—who was present. By 1660, they were fifty thousand strong.

As they trusted the Spirit to guide them, the Quakers forsook ritual, denounced sin, refused violence, swore off oaths, and withheld tithes to the Church of England. For this, they were persecuted and Fox was often imprisoned. Still, the movement spread to Europe and North America. And their hearing from God rooted them, like giant yews in a circle. They were among the first white people to denounce slavery starting in the 1670s and were prominently involved in the Underground

Railroad. Quaker women such as Lucretia Mott, Susan B. Anthony, and Alice Paul led the charge for women's right to vote in America. Some of the most recognized justice organizations today—such as Amnesty International and Oxfam—have Quaker entrepreneurs at their roots.

The Society of Friends continues to gather in meeting houses, in a circle or a square, trusting that God can speak to and through anyone, together.

In the UCSD story, our student leaders were deeply set against the merging of the two chapters. We started to pray about it. The first thing I felt led to do was to talk with leaders who were against the merge and listen well to their reasons. The biggest complaint, by far, was that the campus ministry staff had taken away their freshmen ministry from them, and they were angry. They thought it was supposed to be a student-led ministry, and the ministers had made these decisions by fiat, and it angered them.

I (James) apologized on our behalf. I said we were sorry, and that we were willing to listen. It rebuilt some trust.

Then a few months in, we decided to have a time to listen to God together during a leadership meeting. I put an open mic in front of them and asked them all to pray to God. I said that if they heard anything while they were praying, they could come up to the mic and share what they heard.

We had no idea how that was going to go.

But student after student came up and started to share that they felt like God was calling us to merge. That we could have the best of both worlds—evangelism and discipleship—if we came together. I was surprised by the students who had seemed in such opposition to the merge come forward and share that God was prompting them to be in favor of it.

One word from God is worth a thousand sermons.

Afterward, we took an informal straw poll. We had three abstains, but the rest of the student leadership was for merging the North and South chapters.

With such a lopsided vote, we moved forward. When large groups began again in the fall, our fellowship grew from 150 to 225—a few months later. In the following years, under Ryan's leadership, it would balloon to 600, and over 100 students would become followers of Jesus every year.

It was a level-two revival. And it was sparked as we heard Jesus speak to us about how to move forward in strategic ways.

In Acts 13, five leaders of the Antioch community gathered to fast and pray. Even with five, it was ethnically and socioeconomically diverse: Barnabas, a Levite from Cyprus; Simeon was likely dark-skinned, due to his nickname; Lucius, from Cyrene; Manaen, who grew up in the household of Herod the tetrarch; and Saul, a Pharisee from Tarsus with Roman citizenship.

While they were worshiping and fasting, the Lord told them to set apart Barnabas and Saul for new work, and they were sent on the first missionary journey to the Gentiles.

And the Christian faith was no longer a marginal, Jewish sect, but instead it was available for the rest of the world.

Discussion Questions

1. Which of the five questions is most helpful to you in discernment?
2. How have you heard, responded, and debriefed in the past?
3. What is God saying to you now, and what are you going to do about it?

Chapter Eleven

KINGDOM BUILDING

Only he who has no use for the empire is fit to be entrusted with it.
THE ZHUANGZI

But seek first his kingdom and his righteousness, and all these things will be given to you as well.
JESUS OF NAZARETH, MATTHEW 6:33

Recently, my North Carolinian hosts had put me up in a house right along the shores of man-made Lake Norman, a few blocks from Michael Jordan's childhood home. Since the owners were away, I (James) had the place all to myself.

When I woke up in the morning, I looked for some coffee. This may speak of the state of my soul, but when I wake up, caffeine is not optional. I'm not even sure I'm a Christian before my first cup of espresso. Without caffeine, I usually don't act like one.

If I were to make conclusions based on what I saw in the home, it was clear the hosts had thought of every detail. Soaps, towels, shampoo—the place was set up to make me feel very comfortable. So when I went downstairs, I saw almost all that was necessary for a cup of joe: coffee beans in a jar, a burr grinder, a fancy coffee machine. They had even put out a cup, top down, on top of a pile of brown napkins.

But I couldn't find the coffee filters.

It's sad to admit, but I was getting desperate.

I went through every cabinet drawer in that beautiful kitchen. It was hard not to notice: every item in every drawer was perfectly organized. Each drawer even had its own theme: one was dedicated to technology, while another was devoted to candles. And so on.

I wouldn't have been surprised if Martha Stewart herself had been consulted in the organization. But after a long search, I was still empty handed.

When my host came to pick me up for the day, he asked if I had found everything that I needed. I, perhaps too quickly, confessed that I hadn't had any coffee because I couldn't find the filters.

He looked over at the kitchen counters and immediately said, "Here they are."

Those "brown napkins"? Yep, they were the filters.

Coffee filters in my world are white with fan-like ridges. A large wrapper for Reese's peanut butter cups, but bleached. But the filters on this counter were organic brown, and they were cones folded flat.

My hosts had actually thought of everything and placed everything in plain sight. But I missed it.

I had a preconceived notion of what a coffee filter should look like. I overlooked something brown because I was looking for something white. It was a matter of perspective. Or more accurately, a matter of pre-spective—of pre-seeing or pre-thinking. I had assumptions about something, and it eventually affected what I was able to see. That morning, I went without caffeine. But if I were to have a pre-spective in other areas, I wonder what else I'd miss?

For this chapter, we may not be looking for coffee, but when we talk of revival, we are basically seeking the kingdom of God.

But I wonder, as we seek revival and to lead it, what do we carry in our heads or hearts that will make us miss the kingdom? And if we miss the kingdom, what do we end up building instead?

It's here that I want to address the motivations behind revival leadership. Our motivations are a key distinction between building something that glorifies ourselves or something that will honor God. Although the activities may look similar, what we leave in the end will reflect what was in our hearts.

So the distinction is crucial.

Language of the Empire: Uniformity

To help us understand that distinction, let's look at Genesis 11. At this point, we're at the very beginning stages of the biblical narrative, and the

Scriptures tell us what the state of human communication was at the time: "Now the whole world had one language and a common speech."

It's an interesting verse, less for what it says but more for how we interpret it.

In my Western church experience, I've never heard that line preached in a negative light. It's often read as an unqualified positive, as if it's the way the world should be.

They had only one language. They all understand each other, right? Isn't that great?

It would've been great if the whole world spoke one language. I wouldn't have had to take three years of high school French. *Où est la bibliothèque?*

But just because they spoke the same language, and understood each other's words, they still had many instances of misunderstanding. People often weren't seeking to understand but sought to be understood and justified.

They even killed each other. The violence on the planet created such a rotten stench that God was sorry he made us.

Speaking the same language doesn't automatically help us understand each other.

More important, however, is that the biblical author actually didn't offer a judgment about it one way or the other. He doesn't say that "it was good," like in Genesis 1. At best, it seems neutral in the text, yet we in the Western world often see this speaking of one language as a completely good thing. Perhaps we're seeing the text through white coffee filters?

And what if the text wasn't an unqualified positive but potentially negative? Would that give us a different read?

I'm more of a Star Wars fan, but here's something for the Trekkies. In *Star Trek: The Next Generation*, Starfleet had a tough nemesis: the Borg. They were a group of cybernetic organisms who were all connected to a hive mind called the Collective. Through a process of assimilation, they co-opted the technology and knowledge of other alien species by injecting nanoprobes into their bodies.

Their goal: achieving perfection.

They had a phrase they would say when meeting a new alien race that has Trekkies shuddering in a tizzy of delight: "We are the Borg. Lower your shields and surrender your ships. We will add your biological and technological distinctiveness to our own. Your culture will adapt to service us. Resistance is futile."

In this example, speaking one language isn't a positive idea. For those who grew up in oppressed people groups, the idea of speaking one language could be connected to something more sinister. It's something that a dominant group demands of another, forcing it on them. One language can often be the language of oppression.

The Jewish people, the primary audience of this text, were also often oppressed. At first, it was Egypt. Then Assyria, Babylon, and the Romans. So much of the Scriptures were written while they were oppressed in some way. So perhaps this idea of one language might not be a good thing after all.

History is filled with examples of this kind of imperialism. European colonialists found their way into parts of South America, Africa, and Asia. When the indigenous peoples were forced to stop speaking their own tongues for the one tongue, it probably didn't feel great. In the Americas, Native Americans were stripped of their cultures and languages, their children forced to attend schools where they would be beaten if they spoke their tribal languages. Captain Richard H. Pratt, the founder of the Carlisle Indian Industrial School in Pennsylvania, wanted to educate Native Americans in an enlightened view compared to his contemporaries, yet he still had a philosophy that dominated his style of education: "Kill the Indian, and save the man."

They forced them to speak one language.

To add support for this point of view, we turn to the end of the Scriptures. In Revelation 7:9, we are given a picture of heaven: "After this I looked, and there before me was a great multitude that no one could count, from every nation, tribe, people and language, standing before the throne and before the Lamb."

Heaven is very diverse. Multiple languages find expression. Although unified in worship to the King, uniformity is absent. All of our linguo-cultural differences come before the throne, and this takes place in heaven, so all of it is good and intended.

In heaven, we don't all speak one language.

Uniformity often serves those who are in power. If we have privilege, then much can be accomplished under one language. But from this perspective, speaking one language could be less of a good thing, and more in line with the ways of the empire.

In the dictionary, an empire is "an extensive group of states or countries under a single supreme authority." It's about power and control. It's about using the tools at our disposal to stay in charge and keep others in check. And if we're building an empire, we'll want to be people at the top of an organization—that's also at the top of the culture as well. Empire is hegemony, and it seeks uniformity.

The kingdom of God, however, is of love and service. Jesus said this to his disciples:

> You know that the rulers of the Gentiles lord it over them, and their high officials exercise authority over them. Not so with you. Instead, whoever wants to become great among you must be your servant, and whoever wants to be first must be your slave—just as the Son of Man did not come to be served, but to serve, and to give his life as a ransom for many.

Desires of the Empire: Significance and Security

There are many reasons that people want to build empires instead. As we continue in Genesis 11:3-4, the builders of Babel have the technology to bake bricks. They not only find progress in their construction skills but they also find hubris: "Come, let us build ourselves a city, with a tower that reaches to the heavens, so that we may make a name for ourselves; otherwise we will be scattered over the face of the whole earth."

The folks of Babel want to build a city. And city building, in and of itself, isn't bad. But in this passage, the reasons why people are building this city aren't neutral. Even if it might benefit the people of the city, they build in a way that sets them against the wishes and will of God.

How do we know that? Back in Genesis 1:28, God gives the people specific commands: "God blessed them and said to them, 'Be fruitful and increase in number; fill the earth and subdue it.'"

Among other things, they were to fill the earth. God's intention was that the people of God would scatter throughout the face of the earth and multiply.

Healthy, living things multiply. But some large corporations alter the genetic makeup of seeds so they can't multiply. They sell this seed to farmers, who can't then use the crop to sustain a next generation, and in so doing, the corporations secure funding, since farmers will have to pay for the seed in every growing season.

It's a form of enslavement, of empire. Some farmers are killing themselves in protest to this injustice.

The act of multiplication generally happens one baby at a time, although you might have twins. Regardless, in each baby, generally, is the potential for the next generation. And when that gets compounded, well, exponentially, you are at the cusp of explosive growth. Life is entrusted to the next generation, who then multiplies to create the next.

Spiritually, this is what revival looks like.

At Babel, this was supposed to happen: healthy scattering and exponential multiplication.

But they do something else. In building their empire, they ask, How can we make a name for ourselves and not be scattered? How can we be famous and safe? How can we have significance and security? How can we make sure to find it, and build this city and tower for ourselves, for our name and our sake?

It's about building things for our satisfaction, instead of God's glory.

How does empire thinking creep into our kingdom thinking? Empire thinking and kingdom thinking can look similar in terms of behavior and even short-term results. It's not always easy to discern in the moment what is of the kingdom of what is of the empire.

For example, InterVarsity's 2030 Calling is huge. But as we chase this dream, we are often tempted to empire thinking.

Sometimes, we can sink into our own pond of hubris. Inter-Varsity has a particular kingdom flavor: we've been doing multiethnic ministry since the 1940s with integrated Bible studies and camps when that was a dangerous thing to do. We love our Scripture study method—the manuscript study. We love reaching not just the students of the university but also graduate students and faculty. We want to redeem not just the people but the ideas and structures of the university.

We don't just want to fish in the pond but to take care of the whole pond.

And this vision, in our arrogance, can quickly become about us. We can raise the banner of InterVarsity high. It's about our name. Always be wary of a ministry that talks more about itself than it talks about Jesus. About our version of Christianity. And we can try to tackle the other campuses—the other 1,800 campuses—on our own.

We'll make a tower that reaches to the heavens. We'll be such a juggernaut that we won't be scattered. We'll have power and influence. We can control our brand.

But instead, we're partnering with Cru, The Navigators, Pulse, and other campus ministries to reach the campuses we're not yet on. We've built everycampus.com together to mobilize prayer for every campus. We're speaking at each other's conferences and sharing resources. And we hope to build something that is less about our empires and something greater for the kingdom.

It's easy to identify with our ministries. But in what ways do you derive your sense of significance from your ministry? In what ways does it serve your empire rather than the kingdom? In what ways do you seek security from your empire rather than generously unloading the resources for the sake of all the kingdom?

We have to be constantly on guard. The empire always strikes back, but the kingdom always gives back.

Empire building rarely goes our way, anyway. We often want to make a name for ourselves and not be scattered. We are tempted to take control and make ourselves significant and secure. But in this passage, even though they build a tower that reaches to the heavens, God still has to come down to see it built.

It's a great irony; we think it's going to be great, but it is still small in God's eyes. He's doing something far bigger.

In the rest of this passage, God puts them back on track, back to "scattering." God confuses their language so they can get back to it. It's a severe mercy. But more importantly, languages—and their related terms of ethnicities and cultures—were not a curse.

We won't find language like that in this chapter.

Culture is a gift.

And in the following chapter, God makes a promise to Abraham, the father of the Jewish people. God would make his name great and his descendants would be as numerous as the grains of sand on the shore.

He merely needed to trust God with everything he was and all that he had.

Give up the empire and seek the kingdom.

Empire Building vs. Kingdom Seeking: How Do You Know?

In empire-building and kingdom-seeking, the activities can feel similar. So how do we know if we're on the right track? Here are three questions to help us think about it as we long for revival.

Making our name great. The first temptation is to bend revival to meet our own selfish needs. We might hope that it will leave the legacy we've always dreamed of leaving. Perhaps we want history to have its eyes on us, written in history books for later generations of revival leaders to praise. Our dreams for our ministry could be muddled with delusions of grandeur. So beware the church or faith community that talks about itself more than Jesus. The main question: When you grow or multiply, does it have to be led by your community and have your branding, or do you partner well with and purposely learn from others?

So we won't be scattered. The second temptation is to twist revival into helping us feel secure. We want a large enough ministry that would support a lavish lifestyle. We want to be in the kingdom, but we often want the perks of the world. We want to make sure we succeed, but sometimes it's at the expense of others or the communities that we serve. The main question: Is your heart primarily for the welfare of your ministry or for the welfare of the communities or regions in which you serve?

God comes down. The third temptation is to seek revival in our own strength and effort. This will certainly fail. We will find ourselves burned out, trying to accomplish what only God can do. The main question: Are you tired and jaded because of your own strength, or do you still have a sense of wonder at what God might do?

We don't have to create our own security and significance. That's the way to lose these things. We don't seek these things on our own without detriment to our souls.

Instead, God will give us these things. "Seek first his kingdom ... and all these things will be given to you."

Dying To It All

Many years ago, I (James) was conned into playing a board game called Risk. It's a game about world domination, and each player represents an army. Players battle until there is one dictator left, ruling over the world.

It's a painful game for me. I always lose.

It's because I happen to be the owner of a trash-talking mouth. If I'm doing anything competitive, my tongue gets me into trouble. I really can't help it. So in a game like Risk, you may as well put a giant bull's-eye on my forehead and tell everyone to shoot. And since this game is more than a three-hour commitment, I don't just lose, but I lose slowly and painfully.

I hate this game.

But playing with noncompetitive people makes it worse. I had a friend who really didn't care if he won or not, but he loved taking someone down with him. So he attacked at will, without rhyme or reason.

As a result, the tenor of the game changed: we had to curry his favor. If he decided that he would send all of his green troops against my little yellow formations, I knew I would be done. The other three players knew this too, and suddenly, for a player who didn't care if he won or lost, he found himself with a great deal of power. When he didn't care about winning for himself, he had incredible influence to sway the game.

If we're willing to die, we can truly live. We often hold too tightly to our comfortable way of life. I know I do.

Sacrifice? Can we talk about that over a cup of Starbucks?

But if we truly stopped trying to win the game of life by our culture's rules—Most stuff? Largest ministry? Widest fame?—perhaps we could actually influence the world around us. If we "died" each day, perhaps we would help others find life. And we would also find life for ourselves as well as meaning and purpose to live by.

Jesus did. He put everything on the line for the cause, so much so that he endured a hellish and torturous death. His life wasn't above the cause, so he laid it down. Willingly. He made the ultimate sacrifice, and he moved the world.

Others followed his example, laying down their own empires. Whether they had names like Nikolaus Ludwig von Zinzendorf or Aimee Semple McPherson or Simeoni Nsibambi, or had movements known as the Methodists or the Pentecostals or the Pyongyang revivals—they tried to seek first his kingdom with all of their lives.

As revived leaders, they saw revivals in their time. And they will be swept up into a larger story. One day, everything will be made right. All that is outside the will of God will cease. A new heaven and a new earth will be made.

Until then, we long for revival in our day.

But we have to stop trying to win the game. The one who wants to be great, must serve. We have to lose our life to find it.

Discussion Questions

1. In what ways are you tempted to build an empire?
2. In what ways are you being called to learn from or partner with others?
3. What is something that God is calling you to die to, so that you can more fully live?

Outro

ALREADY AND NOT YET

I just want us to realize that we are in the day of small things. But there are big things, and I am talking about the longing for these bigger things.
MARTYN LLOYD-JONES, *REVIVAL*

Now to him who is able to do immeasurably more than all we ask or imagine, according to his power that is at work within us, to him be glory in the church and in Christ Jesus throughout all generations, for ever and ever!
PAUL OF TARSUS, EPHESIANS 3:20-21

A painting collected dust in an attic for more than a century. The fast brushstrokes of gold and green hint at a stony heath, twisted oaks, wheat fields, and a ruin on a French hill. When peeking through the foliage, a faint blue on the horizon marks the Mediterranean Sea. Small pillows of white dot the blue sky.

In 1908, a Paris art dealer sold it to a Norwegian industrialist, Christian Nicolai Mustad. But when a business rival, who also was an art collector, came for a visit, he declared the painting a fake. Embarrassed, Mustad had it banished to the attic.

There it languished until his death in 1970, and another set of owners bought it from his estate. They had it examined again in 1991, but it was still rejected. In 2011, however, new techniques for identifying and authenticating paintings emerged. So the painting was brought to authorities yet again.

After two long years, looking at the composition of the paint, the makeup of the canvas, and corroborating historical evidence, they finally conceded the truth.

It was an actual Van Gogh. And not just any Van Gogh. "Sunset at Montmajour" was painted in 1888, which is considered the most important period of his life, when he created other masterpieces like his still lifes with sunflowers, "The Yellow House," and "The Bedroom in Arles." Up until 1901, it was in his brother's collection. It was then sold to a Parisian art dealer, who sold it seven years later to Mustad. It's worth tens of millions. Comparable Van Gogh paintings sold at auction went for $40 million to $80 million.

What if revival is our painting in the attic? What if revival is a concept collecting dust in our lives, because we thought we were looking at a fake?

If "global revivals are at the heart of the global resurgence of Christianity," perhaps revival is worth another look.

At the start of this book, I (James) wrote about my hatred for the word *revival*. I didn't understand why we used that word all the time in my Korean American immigrant church.

I get it now.

In 1903, a Canadian physician and Methodist missionary, R.A. Hardie, was burned out. He worked hard, but he hadn't seen much fruit. So he began to examine the state of his soul.

During this period, he gathered with seven other missionaries for a week-long conference in Wonsan, a port city on the coast directly east of Pyongyang. Through studying Luke

11:13, "How much more will your Father in heaven give the Holy Spirit to those who ask him!" he realized that he had served far too much under his own effort.

He felt a deep conviction of sin, and a profound sense of God's holiness. Then he felt the Spirit's peace and power rush into him. That's a level-one personal revival.

When he later retold this story to a Korean congregation, they were inspired. Afterward, they sought the gift of the Spirit, led Bible studies, held prayer meetings, confessed their sins, gave testimonies, and experienced the presence of God in powerful and intimate ways. A level-two communal revival was underway.

The meetings started to grow, and revival spread throughout the Wonsan area. By 1906, similar revivals were breaking out in Seoul, and they had caught wind of the Welsh Revivals and another revival in India. A level-three regional revival grew.

Then news of the Wonsan revivals reached Pyongyang. There, Presbyterian missionaries began to seek spiritual gifts, as they had been given in Wonsan.

In January 1907, 960 had registered for a ten-day conference at the largest church in Korea at that time, the First Church of Pyongyang. During the day, they studied the Scriptures. The evenings, however, were open to the public, where about 1,500 gathered.

On the evening of January 14, 1907, Presbyterian missionary William Blair preached, and Graham Lee led the time of prayer. He called everyone to pray, even aloud if they wished.

The room burst into "a roar of prayer."

The Holy Spirit fell on the people, and they publicly confessed their sins. They forgave and reconciled with each other. In a time when the country was under harsh Japanese rule and independence movements fell apart, people looked to God for hope. William Blair, in his book *The Korean Pentecost*, put it this way:

> The effect was indescribable—not of confusion, but a vast harmony of sound and spirit, a mingling together of souls moved by an

irresistible impulse of prayer. The prayer sounded to me like the falling of many waters, an ocean of prayer beating against God's throne. It was not many, but one, born of one Spirit, lifted to one Father above.

The next morning, Gil Seon-Ju, who is considered by many to be the father of Korean Christianity, said this apt word the following morning: "This is what revival does. It tears away your sins and sets you free."

From here, many churches would be planted throughout the nation—and a level-four national revival began.

But this is where the story gets personal.

A missionary connected to the Pyongyang revivals was sent over fifty miles north to a little town called Yongmi in the Bakchon region. He met a shaman, Hyun Doo Shin, who was going through her own crisis of faith. She served at a tree shrine where the villagers worshiped, but her first two children had succumbed to early deaths. She was irate; she had devoted her entire life to this tree spirit, but in return, it did nothing to save her children. So she took out her anger and frustration on that spirit.

She uprooted the tree.

It was right around this time that she met the missionary. He told her about Jesus and invited her to follow him. She responded and gave her life to him. And naturally, as the spiritual leader, she told her village about her newfound faith.

The entire village came to faith and a church was born.

That shaman-turned-church-planter was my great-great-grandmother. Her son, my great-grandfather, was an elder at that church. My grandfather and grandmother met in the same church, and in the early 1940s, my dad, as an infant, was baptized there.

Over the generations, that village became a town. On Sundays, my dad remembers that not a single store would be open.

My grandfather was a deacon at that church and, because of his Christian faith, was also an activist. His faith pitted him against the growing power of the Communists, which brought him persecution. They put him in jail, but my grandmother bribed the guards to secure his release. But when the Korean War broke out, the Communists poured in from the north. When the radio went silent, my family knew they had to run. They would narrowly escape south across the Han River and headed all the way down to Pusan.

There, my grandfather planted a church with some friends. When they moved to Seoul four years later, my grandfather planted another church with some friends. Both churches still exist today.

My parents immigrated to America and eventually made their way to Seattle, where I grew up. There, they helped a fledgling church plant blossom, which still thrives today.

Then I was sent to Boston. I thought I was going to go to college, but little did I know that I would also be training for ministry. After college, I helped plant a church in an urban part of greater Boston. Twenty-two years later, that church also still serves in its community.

And now, as a leader in a national ministry, which is connected to a larger global movement, I long for revival.

But revival, at least for my family, has come full circle. Our spiritual history has its origins in the Pyongyang revivals of 1907. And the reason I heard the word revival constantly in the Korean immigrant church is because that's how the Korean Protestant church was born. Even our style of prayer—out loud, all at once—came from those revivals. Revival gave the Korean faith community courage to stay strong during both Japanese and Communist persecution, and now their congregations are the largest in the world. From there, many Korean immigrant churches were planted overseas, helping many people come to faith and grow in Jesus—a level-five global revival.

More personally, my parents—direct spiritual descendants of revival—showed me, by their example, how to live out my faith. If I am half the man my dad is when I am his age, then my life will be a success. They received faith from their parents, who forged theirs through the fires of persecution—my Korean grandparents fluently spoke the language of their oppressors, Japanese. And they learned faith from their parents, who found their souls alive through revivals that swept the country and started their church.

Revival's hands have reached through generations and across the globe to a garage-turned-office just outside of Los Angeles, where I write and pray of passing on the desire to seek revival—

To you.

***

In chapter five, I (Ryan) shared about receiving God's call to seek him for revival in San Diego. I felt led to renew my commitment to campus ministry at the time, and ten years later, it still burns white-hot within me.

But my heart aches when I hear the statistics about the net loss of churches every year in our country. It pains me to see the trends that with each successive generation, from boomers to Xers to millennials to iGens, church attendance decreases. Each generation seems increasingly disconnected from the church as a whole. I found myself back at the beginning of the U curve—Stage 1: holy discontent.

So, after twenty-one years of campus ministry, I felt God leading me into pastoral leadership at my local church.

Back in 1997, when I first stepped foot on the UCSD campus as a green-behind-the-ears InterVarsity staff worker, the first wave of millennials was just washing up on the shores of university campuses all over our country. I have been ministering to this generational cohort for the past twenty years. Now, with the last of the millennials out of college and into society at large, I feel called to follow them into the local church. My hope is to help the church know how to receive the best this generation has to offer to the church, and to offer something from the wisdom and experience of the previous generation.

I see the Spirit creating an intergenerational movement of white-hot lovers of Jesus, clasping hands as we cry out to God together for another mighty movement of his Spirit. It's up to every generation to face the challenges of its time by learning to seek God for his breakthrough. As an Xer, I hope to be a bridge between what God has done and the next mighty wave of God's Spirit.

And I sense that what's needed is not simply a new weekend service strategy or a new way of organizing the church into house cells, satellite campuses, or missional communities, although I see merit in all these approaches. We need something that gets far deeper, closer to the root.

We need revival.

Once again, I find myself at the top of the U curve—Stage 2: untested faith—inspired with fresh vision and fueled by deep, holy discontent. I know there are dark valleys ahead where my faith will be tested, perhaps a Stage 3: crucified hope. I hope and pray that I will have the strength for Stage 4: crisis of faith.

But I also know I'm not alone.

Many others are responding to the Spirit's prompting to seek God for revival. A dear and respected millennial coworker at my church, Kelly Steele, has been on a similar journey—to long for revival. She has gathered a rag-tag group of boomers, Xers, and millennials on Wednesday mornings to seek God.

Every week, for an hour and a half, we pray for revival.

It's a microcosm of the vision God has given me. We pray for the fire to burn brighter in one another, we pray for those who don't yet know Jesus, we cry out from places of deep holy longing, we stoke hope in one another when discouragement threatens to overcome, we pray in spiritual languages, and we pray for healing.

Even though I feel the burden of the church's need for revival, I really don't know how God is going to fulfill the vision he shared with me years ago. Although that calling remains, I don't know how this is all going to work out. I can't control or predict it. I am surrendered to the mystery, even if I don't have any strategies for this season ahead of me.

I hope that I will find myself in Stage 5: revived hope, and eventually—hopefully—on to Stage 6: breakthrough faith.

Until then, I am still contending.

***

And there are ebbs and flows.

The fellowship at UCSD that we've featured prominently in this book had around a dozen years of flow. But now it's starting to show signs of an ebb. Some parts of our ministry are flourishing while others show harder times.

Until the kingdom comes, our faith—as we carry it—always leaks. Slowly or quickly, our faith's vitality, if left to itself, will tend to fade.

So we continue to consecrate. We keep on listening for our next call. We contend for the things we've heard. We pray and train so that our character will hold up. We continue to seek God. We continue to long for revival.

And we don't long for it just because it's extraordinary or special. It's actually the way things should be. Richard Lovelace describes Jonathan Edwards's theology of revival: "Rather it is an outpouring of the Holy Spirit which restores the people of God to normal spiritual life after a period of corporate declension."

It's a new normal, or it's getting us back to what should be normal.

May the Lord bless you as you grapple with your holy discontent, and may he lead you on to breakthrough faith.

May he bring together a group of people—a remnant—that will consecrate themselves, so that you can hear your call, contend for the things you have heard, and ask for the Lord to give you everything you need to have your character become more like Jesus.

May you learn to empower each other, be open to both God's leading in mystery and strategy, discern together the voice of the Lord, and seek not your own empires but instead, seek first the kingdom.

When history closes its final pages, Jesus will be there, where revivals no longer ebb and flow, but remain. Where expectancy finds its fullness.

Along the way, revival isn't something we can manufacture or conjure up. It's not something out of the blue, nor is it random. It isn't a left turn or an outlier dot on the graph of history. It's always initiated by God, and it's always in the cosmic flow of where God is leading the universe.

Revival is where we end up. It's the renewal of all things, an unending revival.

Jesus said, "Look, I am making everything new!" He's done it before. He's doing it now, and he'll do it again at the end.

So for now, we can get ready and be prepared.

For a season of breakthrough.

Word. Deed. Power.

To seek a new normal.

Experiencing the kingdom with all its fullness and fruitfulness.

Praying that heaven would intersect earth.

So that one day all would be made new.

Discussion Questions

1. What is God saying to you about your part in revival?
2. Who is God asking you to long for revival with?

3. What is God asking you to do next?

ACKNOWLEDGMENTS

We have many to thank. We're grateful sojourners of our tribe—InterVarsity Christian Fellowship USA. You all keep challenging us to have a broader view of the gospel and the kingdom, and you've left an indelible mark on our faith. It's still amazing to us that the National Leadership Team embraced revival for our 2030 Calling. We're thankful that we're longing for revival together.

InterVarsity's National Council of Evangelists was an early revival laboratory, and we're grateful for their input and encouragement: Linson Daniel, Bryan Enderle, Rick Mattson, Serene Neddenriep, Doug Schaupp, and York Moore. Out of this group, Doug and Serene—along with other anonymous readers—gave us sharp and frank feedback that made this book so, so much better. Also, the InterVarsity NISET Revival Leadership course gave us a joyful, yet powerful, playground to try out the book's central ideas: Cristina Chapelle, Andrew Givens, Jennifer Hagin,

Andrew Kim, Jessica Marotte, Taylor Rodemoyer, and Shelley Scott.

We also want to thank the good folks in InterVarsity San Diego, where we met. They have a fun, loud, and risk-taking spirit, and a lot of what's in this book has been because of the ways you all have loved, supported, and partnered alongside us.

And we owe much to InterVarsity Press. Al Hsu is an ever-present help, although I (James) missed the sarcastic quips that used to come from his editing of previous books. We're thankful for the support from publisher Jeff Crosby, the marketing crew including Christina Gilliland and Andrew Bronson, and the rest of the team at InterVarsity Press—from proofreading to design to distribution. Thank you for all that you do!

From James:

There are people who took the risk with me to make the power circle larger in InterVarsity: Jen Huerta Ball (who also prayed my firstborn into being—I miss you dearly), Charlene Brown,

James Chambers, Lisa Espinelli Chinn, Andrew Givens, Steve Marks, Serene Neddenriep, Maghan Perez, Paul Rapley, Rick Richardson, Lina Sánchez-Herrera, Jordan Seng, Noemi Vega Quiñones, and Nicole Voelkel. And I'm thankful to all of the NISET Holy Spirit and Witness (now Holy Spirit on Campus) alumni who continue to seek the intersection of mystery and strategy.

The Strategy & Innovation Team constantly helps me dream in bigger and more unexpected ways, and regularly presses me into revival: Scott Bessenecker, Bethany Horvath, Maureen Huang, Anna Lee-Winans, Doug Schaupp, and Shawn Young. Grace Hayashi, who is also on that team and serves as my assistant, is exceptionally gifted, has a serving heart, and doesn't wait to roll up her sleeves to get things done. There's no way I survive a working week without her skillful and prayerful help!

A shout-out to the Vineyard Underground. We sought the intersection of word, deed, and power together, and I'm grateful for all of you who were part of it. A special thanks to those who led in the community when we were together. I miss you guys: Beau and Kristina Crosetto, Duke and Erin Han, Nick and Natalia Kwok, Steve and Larissa Marks, Keith and Joanie Le, and Cerina Epple. I'm still hitting tennis balls with Nick, and that has its own way of keeping me sane.

My church home, Gardena Valley Baptist Church, knows how to support and encourage people, especially when they're grieving. They've been alongside my family in the toughest years in our lives, and they make faith compelling enough that my kids still want to go to church. There's too many to thank there as well, but Stephen and Nancy Langley were a big reason why we came, and Doug and Sue Brown are a big reason why we stay. Plus, a thank you to Michelle Law, Tammy Hernandez, Emily Noguchi, and the volunteers who pour into our children—my wife and I don't take that for granted.

My advisory council helps me solve my leadership problems while just being great friends of heart and soul: Doug Creviston, Aimee Baek, Mark Gustafson, Aaron Hernandez, Ken Kawahara, Jon

Kohl, Winston Lai, and Caroline Rhim. And to my other ministry partners—I wish I could name you all here—your generosity and prayers are fuel for the fire.

My family makes this work possible and this life enjoyable. My parents, Peter and Linda Choung, are so loving and giving, often watching our kids and praying for me even more. Isaiah, Nathan, and Jamie—I love who you are and who you're becoming. And I'm thankful for every day I get to be with the love of my life, Jinhee. She's her namesake—so much truth and joy to me! I hope we get many more days ahead. But no expectations, just expectancy.

From Ryan:

Above all, Stacy, my bride and my co-laborer in seeking God for revival—I never could have faithfully pursued my calling without your incredible gift of faith, indefatigable support, and endless brainstorming conversations. You kept me from quitting.

Mark Slomka—my first and always pastor, who stoked the flame of revival in my heart over twenty years ago and still does today.

Tom, Rob, Tracey, and Eddie—we sought God for revival together, and I am truly grateful for your friendship and partnership in the trenches. And to all the InterVarsity staff and students in SoCal and my beloved San Diego who gave themselves wholeheartedly along the way.

Jennifer Huerta Ball—a true revival leader. I will always carry your riotous laughter and prophetic voice with me in my heart.

Greg and Sarah—for your input, deep conversations, and shared vision for campus, church, and culture.

Patrice—thank you for all your prayers and help in the writing process. You are the real deal and have inspired me toward amazing breakthroughs.

My parents and siblings—thank you for following Jesus alongside me—with all of its joys and sorrows—and for inspiring others with our family's revival story.

Eric and Kandi—your revival leadership changed the course of my life and ministry. Thank you for wading into the river with me that day in 2009. Go Carl!

My grafted Gerry, Howald, and Lloreda families—thank you for your warm embraces and reliable love in all seasons. And those of you who served as undercover prayer operatives throughout this book-writing project, thank you for lifting up my needs before I even knew them each day on your morning walks with Jesus.

Thank you to the Bowmans, Butlers, and Vicks who have supported and walked alongside our family when we found ourselves at the bottom of the U curve. Your faith carried us up and out on so many occasions. If everyone had friends like you, the world would have many more breakthroughs!

Thank you, Payson, for leading me to faith back in high school. You helped lead me into the most important breakthrough of my life. And to Andy, Mark, Dan, and Phil—through you I got my first taste of revival.

To all our faithful ministry partners—while your names are too many to list here, your impact is no less felt. I'm thankful that I have not been called to revival alone but in the context of the community and gracious accountability you all have provided.

Bill and Jami—thank you for cheering me and my family on over these past five years. Thank you for leading us beside green pastures and providing a feast in the midst of our enemies.

Finally, I'm thankful for North Coast Calvary Chapel, the new faith community I get to seek revival with. Thank you for receiving me with such open hearts and for your eagerness to seek God for more! A shout-out to the Wednesday morning revival prayer crew!

From both:

We are grateful for each other too! We've been like brothers in the ups and downs of family and ministry life, first as campus ministers together at UCSD, continuing through ministry in San Diego, and then back again in the evangelism department. We've had many other times of intersection, which included a trip to Prague where we were inspired by campus evangelists from twenty-five European countries—and there started to dream about how our San Diego–born partnership could blossom into something more. We're thankful that God kept throwing us together, and our lives are richer for it.

And of course, we thank Jesus. As we wrote this book, we found times when we were stuck, and other times when we were giddy with encouragement. But we often found ourselves thankful that Jesus reached out to us and invited us to follow him. We would be wrecks without his mercy and grace. Instead, we find ourselves as grateful pilgrims, seeking the kingdom and longing for revival.

NOTES

Intro: Why Revival?

Revival meeting: The Korean word for revival meeting is 부흥회 (bu-heung-hwae).

How many "prophets": If you were a prophet during Old Testament times, and you gave a prophecy that didn't come to pass, they were supposed to stone you (Deuteronomy 18:20-22).

All these people: Hebrews 11:13.

faithful: Merriam-Webster, s.v. "faithful (*adj.*)," accessed May 21, 2019, www.merriam-webster.com/dictionary/faithful.

a long obedience: Eugene Peterson, *A Long Obedience in the Same Direction,* commemorative ed. (Downers Grove, IL: InterVarsity Press, 2019).

Hope is a dangerous thing: The Shawshank Redemption, directed by

Frank Darabont (New York: Castle Rock Entertainment, 1994).

Please, man of God: 2 Kings 4:16.

Did I ask you: 2 Kings 4:28.

Hope deferred: Proverbs 13:12.

Now faith is confidence: Hebrews 11:1-2.

Aren't revivals quirky folk rituals: Mark R. Shaw, *Global Awakening: How 20th Century Revivals Triggered a Christian Revolution* (Downers Grove, IL: InterVarsity Press, 2010), 12.

We catalyze movements: If you want to learn more about InterVarsity's 2030 Calling, check this out: https://intervarsity.org/intervarsitys-2030-calling. Also, if you want to be involved in praying for a campus without a witnessing community, see: https://everycampus.com.

Will you not revive: Psalm 85:6.

Every major advance of the kingdom: Richard Lovelace, *Dynamics of Spiritual Life* (Downers Grove, IL: InterVarsity Press, 1979), 22.

Its center has shifted away: Philip Jenkins, *The Next Christendom: The Coming of Global Christianity,* 3rd ed. (New York: Oxford University Press, 2011), 1-2.

Global revivals: Shaw, *Global Awakening,* 12.

Pop albums are titled Revival: Selena Gomez released hers in October 2015, Eminem, in December 2017.

We need form and fire: John Mark Comer and Mark Sayers, "The Portland Sessions: Part 6," *This Cultural Moment,* March 19, 2019. https://thisculturalmoment.podbean.com/e/the-portland-sessions-part-6/ (accessed March 29, 2019).

1. Revival for the Rest of Us

Renewal, revival and awakening: Richard Lovelace, *Dynamics of Spiritual Life* (Downers Grove, IL: InterVarsity Press, 1979), 22.

a renewed conviction: Charles Finney, *Experiencing Revival* (New Kensington, PA: Whitaker House, 1984), 11.

a period of unusual blessing: Martyn Lloyd-Jones, *Revival* (Westchester, IL: Crossway Books, 1987), 99.

faith becomes "white-hot": Steve Addison, *Movements That Change the World* (Downers Grove, IL: InterVarsity Press, 2011), 38. He shares that all revivals start with "white-hot" faith.

Large numbers of persons: James Burns, *Revival: Their Laws and Leaders* (Grand Rapids: Baker Book House, 1960), originally printed in 1909, 21.

A season in which: Timothy Keller, *Center Church: Doing Balanced*

Gospel-Centered Ministry in the City (Grand Rapids: Zondervan, 2012), 54.

broad-scale movements: Lovelace, *Dynamics of Spiritual Life,* 22.

Global revivals are charismatic people movements: Mark R. Shaw, *Global Awakening: How 20th Century Revivals Triggered a Christian Revolution* (Downers Grove, IL: InterVarsity Press, 2010), 17.

a definition for revival: The friends and colleagues who helped us come to this definition sat on InterVarsity's Council of National Evangelists, which included Linson Daniel, Bryan Enderle, Rick Mattson, Serene Neddenriep, Doug Schaupp, York Moore, and the authors.

are at the heart: Shaw, *Global Awakening,* 12.

In Word, Deed, and Power: Sam Metcalf's 2014 monograph titled *Word, Deed, Power: The Three Dimensions of the Gospel* is a helpful resource. See https://churchnext.info/assets/resource

s/booklets/metcalf/cn_booklet_metcalf_1.pdf.

Therefore I glory in Christ Jesus: Romans 15:17-19, emphasis ours.

from Jerusalem all the way: Douglas J. Moo, *The Epistle to the Romans,* The New International Commentary on the New Testament (Grand Rapids: William B. Eerdmans Company, 1996), 896.

to relate fully: J.P. Louw & E.A. Nida, *Greek-English Lexicon of the New Testament: Based on Semantic Domains* (New York: United Bible Societies, 1998).

By word, we mean: We aren't just applying modern sensibilities to these words. See Moo, *The Epistle to the Romans,* 893: "This makes it more likely that 'by the power of the Spirit' refers to all the means of ministry that Paul identifies in vv. 18b-19a. And, while 'the power of signs and wonders' probably relates to the 'deeds' part of Paul's ministry, it is unlikely that Paul intends the phrase as a complete description of his 'work.' For there is no good reason to confine the term 'deed' or 'work' to miraculous works only; and Paul's apostolic 'work' included many other kinds of activities."

a heavenly experience that does no earthly good: A nod to an Oliver Wendell Holmes Sr. quote: "Some people are so heavenly minded that they are no earthly good."

a form of godliness but denying its power: 2 Timothy 3:5.

lay on the ground like dead men: "The Little Flowers of St. Francis," in *St. Francis of Assisi: Writings and Early Biographies:English Omnibus of the Sources for the Life of St. Francis,* edited by Marion A. Habig, 3rd edition (Chicago: Franciscan Herald Press, 1973), 1331.

The Pentecostal movement, as it grew: Unfortunately almost at the outset, white leaders resisted and split the Pentecostal movement. After witnessing this interracial fellowship, a white leader who was invited to the pulpit at Azusa decried that, "God is sick at his stomach!" Douglas J. Nelson, "For Such a Time as This: The Story of Bishop William J. Seymour and the Azusa Street Revival" (PhD diss., University of Birmingham, England, 1981), 209.

a share in the power of Pentecost: J.E. Church, *Quest for the Highest* (Exeter, UK: Paternoster, 1981), 68.

I have never before seen: Church, *Quest for the Highest,* 145.

Those touched by this revival: Thanks to Scott Bessenecker for pointing us to this story.

We use manuscript Bible study: For more information on InterVarsity's manuscript study method, check out: https://intervarsity.org/bible-study (accessed April 20, 2019).

alumni have done amazing things: To learn more about InterVarsity's alumni, go here: https://intervarsity.org/stories?action= (accessed April 20, 2019). In this particular reference, Mark Earley served as Virginia's attorney general but also as the president of Prison Fellowship, while Gary Haugen founded the International Justice Mission.

Do not quench the Spirit: 1 Thessalonians 5:19.

Revivals always start: Malcom McDow and Alvin L. Reid, *Firefall 2.0* (Wake Forest, NC: Gospel Advance Books, 2014), 8-9.

Go home. Lock yourself in your room: Mark Batterson, *The Circle Maker* (Grand Rapids: Zondervan, 2016), 225.

Personal revivals: In their book, *Firefall 2.0,* McDow and Reid outline a similar paradigm of seeing revivals on a gradient from personal to global levels of impact.

In the evening, I went: John Wesley, *The Journal of the Rev. John Wesley* (London: Wesleyan Conference Office, 1903), 1:97.

About three in the morning: Wesley, *The Journal,* 1:160-61.

The fire is kindled: Harry S. Stout, *The Divine Dramatist: George Whitefield and the Rise of Modern Evangelicalism* (Grand Rapids: Eerdmans, 1991), 73-74.

England itself was transformed: Diane Severance, "Evangelical Revival in England," Christianity.com, April 28, 2010, https://www.christianity.com/church/church-history/timeline/1701-1800/evangelical-revival-in-england-11630228.html.

kingdom of God was near: Mark 1:14-15.

Your kingdom come: Matthew 6:10.

a mustard seed: Matthew 13:31-32.

2. From Holy Discontent to Crucified Hope

How long, LORD: Psalm 13:1-2.

Blessed are: Matthew 5:3-10.

Christianity has nothing to say: John Eldredge, *Desire: The Journey We Must Take to Find the Life God Offers* (Nashville: Thomas Nelson, 2007), 43.

Don't waste your pain: Mark Foreman, senior pastor at North Coast Calvary Chapel in Carlsbad, California.

Master, leave: Luke 5:8-10, MSG.

Do not ask: Charles H. Spurgeon, *The Complete Works of C.H. Spurgeon*, vol.48, *Sermons 2760-2811*, sermon 2800. See also https://www.ccel.org/ccel/spurgeon/sermons48.xli.html.

When transformation comes: Eldredge, *Desire*, 35.

What do you want: Mark 10:36.

Today salvation has come: Luke 19:9-10.

Sirs, what must I do: Acts 16:30-31.

households came to faith: Acts 10:1–11:14; 16:14-15; 18:8.

Do not despise these small beginnings: Zechariah 4:10, NLT.

Blessed are you, Simon: Matthew 16:17-19.

Get behind me, Satan: Matthew 16:23.

"to hope" and "to wait": J. Swanson, *Dictionary of Biblical Languages with Semantic Domains: Hebrew (Old Testament)* (Oak Harbor, WA: Logos Research Systems, Inc., 1997), electronic ed. For example, in Isaiah 40:31, the root Hebrew word, *qavah*, is translated "hope" in the NIV, but "wait" in the ESV.

Hope that is seen: Romans 8:24-25.

3. From Crisis of Faith to Breakthrough Faith

difference between expectations and expectancy: Danny Lee Silk, Heaven

Come Conference, Los Angeles, CA, September 22, 2017.

Expectations are resentments under construction: Anne Lamott, *Hallelujah Anyway: Rediscovering Mercy* (New York: Riverhead Books, 2017), 80.

I am ready to go: Luke 22:33.

Abraham ... in hope believed: Romans 4:18-19.

uncertainty, risk: Brown, *Daring Greatly*, 29.

guard your heart: Proverbs 4:23.

Hope is like a reservoir: John Piper, "What is Hope?" Desiring God, April 6,1986, https://www.desiringgod.org/messages/what-is-hope.

You might put it this way: Piper, "What Is Hope?"

Jesus himself came up: Luke 24:15-16.

Cleopas and likely his wife: Victoria Emily Jones, "The Unnamed Emmaus Disciple: Mary, Wife of Cleopas?" *Art & Theology* (blog), April 28, 2017, https://artandtheology.org/2017/04/28/the-unnamed-emmaus-disciple-mary-wife-of-cleopas/. According to Jones, James Montgomery Boice and Jim Cole-Rous think this is the most reasonable interpretation, while Wayne Grudem and N.T. Wright consider it a possibility.

Why are you troubled: Luke 24:37-39.

In Christ and by Christ: A.W. Tozer, *The Knowledge of the Holy* (San Francisco: Harper Collins, 1961), 9.

many convincing proofs: Acts 1:3.

Why are you talking: Mark 8:17-19.

Whoever can be trusted: Luke 16:10.

we might not see a particular breakthrough: Hebrews 11:13, 39. "They did not receive the things promised; they only saw them and welcomed them from a distance, admitting that they were foreigners and strangers on the earth.... These were all commended for their faith, yet none of them received what had been promised."

4. Consecration

set apart the seventh day: Genesis 2:3.

set apart their firstborn: Exodus 13:2.

Moses commanded the Israelites: Exodus 19:10-15.

a consecrating act: Joshua 5:2-9.

Consecrate yourselves: Leviticus 20:7-8.

Consecration is the human side: E.M. Bounds, *The Complete Works of E.M. Bounds on Prayer* (Grand Rapids: Baker Books, 2007), 119.

Make every effort: Hebrews 12:14.

Medieval philosophy had a dictum: Ronald Rolheiser, *The Holy Longing: The Search for a Christian Spirituality* (New York: Doubleday, 1999), 9.

Woe to me: Isaiah 6:5-8.

In a large house: 2 Timothy 2:20-21.

wait for the Holy Spirit: Acts 1:4-8.

God will fill us: Cf. Isaiah 40:31; 64:4.

If your Presence does not go: Exodus 33:1-17.

You have forsaken: Revelation 2:4.

The question is not: Henri Nouwen, *In the Name of Jesus: Reflections on Christian Leadership* (New York: Crossroad Publishing, 1989), 24.

The very act of consecration: Jordan Seng, *Miracle Work: A Down-to-Earth Guide to Supernatural Ministries* (Downers Grove, IL: Inter-Varsity Press, 2013), 67.

Greater love has no one: John 15:13.

For God so loved the world: John 3.16.

are the leaders of the future: Nouwen, *In the Name of Jesus,* 29-30.

whiter than: Mark 9:3.

The disciples had cast out: Matthew 10:1; cf. Luke 9:1-6.

This kind can come out: Mark 9:29.

By connecting self-sacrifice: Seng, *Miracle Work,* 67.

You must realize: Martyn Lloyd-Jones, *Revival* (Westchester, IL: Crossway Books, 1987), 19.

But after a few weeks: Lloyd-Jones, *Revival,* 19.

Well, one day: Lloyd-Jones, *Revival,* 65.

hate in a brother's heart: William N. Blair and Bruce F. Hunt, *The Korean Pentecost and the Sufferings Which*

Followed (1910; repr., Carlisle, PA: Banner of Truth Trust, 1977), 81.

room was full: Blair and Hunt, *The Korean Pentecost,* 83.

Man after man would rise: Blair and Hunt, *The Korean Pentecost,* 84.

Every sin a human being: Blair and Hunt, *The Korean Pentecost,* 87.

largest missionary-sending country: Mark R. Shaw, *Global Awakening: How 20th Century Revivals Triggered a Christian Revolution* (Downers Grove, IL: InterVarsity Press, 2010), 33.

seven spiritual questions: Here's what we call the Seven: 1) In what ways did God make his presence known to you since our last meeting? 2) What do you need to confess since our last meeting? 3) How is your marriage? How are you doing with loving your kids? 4) What opportunities did God give you to serve others since our last meeting? 5) Did God provide an opportunity for you to share your faith with someone? 6) What fruit of the Spirit would you like to see increase in your life? 7) What is God saying to you now, and what will you do about it?

I will not sacrifice: 2 Samuel 24:24.

eagerly seek the greater gifts: 1 Corinthians 12:31.

worldly senses and considerations: Jordan Seng recounted this story to me through email on April 29, 2019.

5. Calling

it is tough enough to serve: Reggie McNeal, *A Work of Heart,* rev. ed. (San Francisco: Jossey-Bass, 2011), 99.

do the things the rabbi did: I heard this phrase from Elizabeth Paul at the Lausanne Younger Leaders Gathering, July 24-26, 2012, Madison, WI.

Very truly I tell you: John 5:19.

We need to learn: Gregg Levoy, *Callings* (New York: Three Rivers Press, 1997), 5.

Luther's views on Jewish people: At first, he seemed to urge a gentle approach in relating to the Jewish people. But as he got older, apparently over his frustrations over their lack of conversion, his views on Jewish people seemed to harden. Cf. Eric W. Gritsch, "Was Luther Anti-Semitic?" *Christianity Today,* https://www.christianitytoday.com/history/issues/issue-39/was-luther-anti-semitic.html (accessed May 6, 2019).

Heidi Baker ... embraced her calling: Heidi Baker, *Birthing the Miraculous* (Lake Mary, FL: Charisma House, 2014), 22.

God is "able to do": Ephesians 3:20.

I will instruct you: Psalm 32:8.

The way of fools: Proverbs 12:15.

We must therefore: Dallas Willard, *Hearing God: Developing a Conversational Relationship with God*, updated and expanded ed. (Downers Grove, IL: InterVarsity Press, 2012), 39.

R-I-S-K: "Quotes from John Wimber," Vineyard USA, accessed July 22, 2019, https://vineyardusa.org/library/quotes-from-john-wimber/.

Ask Him to transform you: Baker, *Birthing the Miraculous*, 40.

Then those who were: Matthew 14:32-33.

6. Contending

Don't waste your time: T.E. Koshy, *Bakht Singh of India* (Downers Grove, IL: Intervarsity Press, 2007), 74.

As he closed in prayer: Koshy, *Bakht Singh*, 74.

the persistent widow: Luke 18:1-8.

Grace is not opposed to effort: Dallas Willard, *The Great Omission: Reclaiming Jesus's Essential Teachings on Discipleship* (New York, NY: HarperCollins, 2006), 61.

He is the one: Colossians 1:28-29.

I have learned: Philippians 4:12.

And will not God: Luke 18:7, emphasis ours.

All night long: Psalm 6:6.

Evening, morning and noon: Psalm 55:17.

LORD, you are: Psalm 88:1.

the Hebrides Revival: Duncan Campbell, "Revival in the Hebrides," The Revival Library, 1968, accessed May 3, 2019, http://www.revival-library.org/index.php/pensketches-menu/historical-revivals/the-hebrides-revival. An actual audio recording of his talk is available online: https://www.youtube.com/watch?v=g8NCXwl0UDg.

There is in our own day: John Piper, *A Hunger for God* (Wheaton, IL: Crossway Books, 1997), 103.

The greatest enemy: Piper, *A Hunger for God,* 14.

Sometimes I would find myself: Charles Finney, *Power from on High,* Kindle ed. (Fort Washington, PA: CLC Publications, 2013), chap.2.

In vain you rise early: Psalm 127:2, 5.

Let us go: Mark 1:38.

7. Character

funny thing about marriages: I must give credit for the story—and the honesty—to Khari Bridgewater.

one of three leaders finishes well: J. Robert Clinton, *Leadership Perspectives: How to Study the Bible for Leadership Insights* (Altadena, CA: Barnabas Publishers, 1993), 93.

I am not like other people: Luke 18:11.

To some who were confident: Luke 18:9.

contempt: Google Dictionary, "Contempt." http://googledictionary.freecollocation.com/meaning?word=contempt.

John Gottman could predict: Malcolm Gladwell, *Blink: The Power of Thinking Without Thinking* (New York: Little, Brown and Company, 2005), 21-22, 32.

Evan himself began: Brynmor Pierce Jones, *An Instrument of Revival: The Complete Life of Evan Roberts 1878-1951* (South Plainfield, NJ: Bridge Publishing, 1995), 87.

the tax collector stood: Luke 18:13.

humility and pride: Andrew Murray, *Humility: The Beauty of Holiness* (Westwood, NJ: Revell, 1966), 12.

This is true humility: Warren, *Purpose Driven Life,* 265.

Those who disregard discipline: Proverbs 15:32.

freedom from the need: David Brooks, *The Road to Character* (New York: Random House, 2015), 8-9.

They radiate: Brooks, *The Road to Character,* xvi.

beast out of the abyss: Paul Wemmer, *Count Zinzendorf and the Spirit of the Moravians* (Maitland, FL: Xulon Press, 2013), 89.

I will pray daily: Wemmer, *Count Zinzendorf,* 120.

Truly I tell you: Luke 18:17.

He humbled himself: Philippians 2:8-9.

8. All Play

the Spirit would be poured out: Joel 2:28-29.

promise was fulfilled in Jerusalem: Acts 2:1-4.

He told them to wait: Acts 1:4-5.

a spiritual gift: 1 Corinthians 12:7.

gifts in evangelism: Ephesians 4:11-13.

called to pray for the sick: Luke 9:1-2; Luke 10:9; 1 Corinthians 12:9; cf. James 5:14.

a new movement would be born: Pew Research Center, "Global Christianity—A Report on the Size and Distribution of the World's Christian Population," http://www.pewforum.org/2011/12/19/global-christianity-movements-and-denominations (accessed January 10, 2019).

When everyone got to play: Rodney Stark, *The Rise of Christianity: How the Obscure, Marginal Jesus Movement*

Became the Dominant Religious Force in the Western World in a Few Centuries (San Francisco: Harper-SanFrancisco, 1997), 3-128. The entire book, a sociologist's perspective on the rapid spread of Christianity, is worth the read.

parable of the sower: Mark 4:3-25.

another agricultural parable: Mark 4:26-29.

farmer is paying attention: A credit to Doug Schaupp for this idea. I've personally heard him say this many times.

Let us go with you: Zechariah 8:23.

Let us consider: Hebrews 10:24-25.

The harvest is plentiful: Luke 10:2.

power and authority: Luke 9:1.

Movements spread: Steve Addison, *Movements That Change the World*

(Downers Grove, IL: InterVarsity Press, 2011), 86.

9. Mystery and Strategy Paradox

paradox: Google Dictionary, http://googledictionary.freecollocation.com/meaning?word=paradox (accessed December 17, 2018).

bear the signet ring: John H. Walton, Victor H. Matthews, and Mark W. Chavalas, *The IVP Bible Background Commentary: Old Testament,* Accordance electronic ed. (Downers Grove, IL: InterVarsity Press, 2000), 473.

great trouble: Nehemiah 1:3.

mourned and fasted: Nehemiah 1:4.

day and night: Nehemiah 1:6.

go straight to strategy: For StrengthsFinder fanatics—we know you're out there!—Strategic is my

(James's) top strength. The second is Woo. Dangerous, right?

expected to shine with joy: Walton, Matthews, and Chavalas, *IVP Bible Background Commentary,* 473.

Why does your face: Nehemiah 2:2.

Culture eats strategy: Andrew Cave, "Culture Eats Strategy for Breakfast. So What's For Lunch?" *Forbes,* November 9, 2017, https://www.forbes.com/sites/andrewcave/2017/11/09/culture-eats-strategy-for-breakfast-so-whats-for-lunch/#5de502f07e0f.

Campus Crusade: Now called Cru. See cru.org.

Three years later: Timothy Keller, "Blueprint for Revival; Introduction 2," Sermon, Redeemer Presbyterian Church, New York, NY, August 5, 1990.

unforced rhythms of grace: Matthew 11:29, MSG.

I was more convinced: James Bryan Smith, *The Good and Beautiful Community: Extending Grace, Demonstrating Love* (Downers Grove, IL: InterVarsity Press, 2010), 139.

ill-defined set of practices: Steve Addison, *Movements That Change the World* (Downers Grove, IL: InterVarsity Press, 2011), 105.

10. Communal Discernment

the key skill: James Choung, *Real Life: A Christianity Worth Living Out* (Downers Grove, IL: InterVarsity Press, 2012), 222.

we learn to discern: Jordan Seng, *Miracle Work: A Down-to-Earth Guide to Supernatural Ministries,* 2nd ed. (Downers Grove, IL: InterVarsity, 2013), 143.

tight editorial control: Seng, *Miracle Work,* 139.

Israel was still under God's covenant: We have to remember that this is specific to the people of Israel, as marked by the Old Testament covenant. Not all things that are promised to Old Testament Israel relates to modern-day Israel, nor does it all apply to the New Testament "Israel," the Christian community.

Don't forget in the darkness: Joe Bayly quoted by Philip Yancey, *Where is God When It Hurts?* (Grand Rapids: Zondervan, 1990), 233.

Listen to me: 2 Chronicles 20:20.

everyone who hears: Matthew 7:24-27.

What is God saying: I (James) heard this phrase from Elizabeth Paul at the Lausanne Younger Leaders Gathering, July 24-26, 2012, Madison, WI.

There is one: George Fox, *George Fox: An Autobiography,* ed. Rufus M. Jones (Philadelphia: Ferris & Leach, 1919), 82.

the Society of Friends (Quakers): Arthur O. Roberts, "George Fox and the Quaker (Friends) Movement," George Fox University, accessed May 6, 2019, https://www.georgefox.edu/about/history/quakers.html.

11. Kingdom Building

brown vs. white: You can apply the metaphor however you'd like.

whole world had one language: Genesis 11:1.

God was sorry he made us: Genesis 6:6.

We are the Borg: Star Trek: First Contact directed by Jonathan Frakes (Los Angeles: Paramount Pictures, 1996).

Kill the Indian: Richard H. Pratt, "Official Report of the Nineteenth Annual Conference of Charities and Correction" (1892), 46–59, accessed May 6, 2019. http://historymatters.gmu.edu/d/4929.

empire: Google Dictionary, "Empire," accessed December 28, 2018. http://googledictionary.freecollocation.com/meaning?word=empire.

whoever wants to be first: Matthew 20:25-28.

farmers are killing themselves: Vandana Shiva, "The Suicide Economy of Corporate Globalization," Countercurrents.org, April 5, 2004, www.countercurrents.org/glo-shiva050404.htm.

God came down: Genesis 11:5.

a severe mercy: Taken from the title of a book by Sheldon Vanauken, *A Severe Mercy* (San Francisco: HarperSanFrancisco, 1992).

Seek first his kingdom: Matthew 6:33.

Risk and dying to it all: This story was previously published on my blog, James Choung, "Boardgames and Sacrifice," jameschoung.net (blog), December 11, 2005, www.jameschoung.net/2005/12/11/boardgames-and-sacrifice.

Outro: Already and Not Yet

Van Gogh in an attic: Mark Brown, "Newly discovered Van Gogh painting kept in Norwegian attic for years," *The Guardian,* September 9, 2013; also, Nina Siegal, "A Van Gogh's Trip From the Attic to the Museum," *The New York Times,* September 9, 2013.

Global revivals are at the heart: Mark R. Shaw, *Global Awakening: How 20th Century Revivals Triggered a Christian Revolution* (Downers Grove, IL: InterVarsity Press, 2010), 12.

Methodist missionary, R.A. Hardie: The Methodist movement itself was born out of John Wesley's revival leadership and the Great Awakenings—a level-five revival.

a roar of prayer: Young-Hoon Lee, "Korean Pentecost: The Great Revival of 1907," *Asian Journal of Pentecostal Studies,* vol.4, no.1, 2001, 76, www.apts.edu/aeimages/File/AJPS_PDF/01-1-yhlee.pdf.

The effect was indescribable: William N. Blair and Bruce F. Hunt, *The Korean Pentecost and the Sufferings Which Followed* (1910; repr., Carlisle, PA: Banner of Truth Trust, 1977), 83-84.

This is what revival does: C. Hope Flinchbaugh, "A Century After North Korean Revival, Dreams of an Encore," *Christianity Today,* January 31, 2007, www.christianitytoday.com/ct/2007/januaryweb-only/105-32.0.html.

My family's escape: If you're interested, you can read more about my family's escape across the Han River in three parts on my website, accessed April 20, 2019, at www.jameschoung.net/2006/12/07/naengmyun-stories-pt-1/.

Korean immigrant churches ... overseas: Soong Chan Rah, *The Next Evangelicalism* (Downers Grove, IL: InterVarsity Press, 2008), 164-79. Rah makes a case that the proliferation of Korean immigrant churches is not only a result of transfer growth but of holistic evangelism. He quotes a 1990 study showing that 70 percent to 77 percent of Korean immigrants actively participate in a Christian church, while in 1991, South Korea was only 25 percent Christian (Korean Overseas Information Service, *A Handbook of Korea* [Seoul, Korea: Ministry of Culture and Information, 1993], 132).

Edwards's theology of revival: Richard Lovelace, *Dynamics of Spiritual Life* (Downers Grove, IL: InterVarsity Press, 1979), 40.

making everything new: Revelation 21:5, NLT.

PRAISE FOR LONGING FOR REVIVAL

"I love spiritually insightful leadership books, and this is a gem! The chapters on the breakthrough U curve will totally change how you approach God with your disappointments and failures. And the genius of the mystery/strategy paradox is worth the price of the book all by itself. Enjoy!"
Doug Schaupp, national director of evangelism, InterVarsity Christian Fellowship, coauthor, *I Once Was Lost* and *Breaking the Huddle*

"In my weaker moments I'm content with mere programs of our own making. But deep down I long to be a part of a genuine work of God. *Longing for Revival* is bursting with the clarity, inspiration, and wise counsel we all need to get involved in what God himself is already doing around us."
Don Everts, author of *The Reluctant Witness* and *The Spiritually Vibrant Home*

"Every generation needs its own revival. My generation of boomers experienced the Jesus movement. We witnessed thousands of counterculture people, who had said *no* to organized religion, say *yes* to radically following Jesus. It's time for a twenty-first-century awakening. These thoughtful pages are filled with hope that may break up the fallow ground and prepare our hearts for a fresh move of heaven."

Mark Foreman, lead pastor of North Coast Calvary Chapel, Carlsbad, California, author of *Wholly Jesus* and *Never Say No*

"James Choung and Ryan Pfeiffer take you on a remarkable journey in *Longing for Revival* by authentically sharing their own search for revival. They share the ups and downs of their faith all the while helping us believe that revival is possible today. If you long to see revival and want to be a part of one, you'll want to read this book!"

Dave Ferguson, lead pastor of Community Christian Church, Naperville, Illinois, and author of *Hero Maker*

"A powerful and must-read primer for anyone longing for revival. Choung and Pfeiffer vulnerably present a thoughtful, biblically grounded framework, without silver bullets or shallow formulas. *Longing for Revival* will inspire and transform not only your leadership but also your faith!"
Tom Lin, president/chief executive officer, InterVarsity Christian Fellowship

"At this time in history, there is a critical need for serious answers to the condition of our world. This book is honest, convincing, hopeful, redemptive, and thorough, and provides a way for every follower of Jesus to become part of the answer, no matter your age and place in life. It is a must-read for every church leader!"
Tammy Dunahoo, vice president of US Operations, the Foursquare Church

"Nothing more is needed in the church other than revival at the present

time. James and Ryan have done us a great service by bringing forth *Longing for Revival.* I strongly believe that this book serves all Christian leaders in all spectrums of leadership, because revival should be the prayer of every church in every part of the world. In *Longing for Revival,* the authors have woven together a vast array of crucial topics of defining revival, experiencing revival, and leading revival. The chapters on the breakthrough U curve have challenged my ways of how I deal with all the frustrations that I am faced with in the ministry that I am leading. The chapter on ministry and strategy has given me insight into how I should reconcile the paradox. I applaud the impact of this book and invite you to read it and join the big rally of longing for revival around the globe."
Robel C. Disasa, general secretary of Evangelical Students Union of Ethiopia (EvaSUE)/IFES-Ethiopia

"This is an amazing book. Ryan Pfeiffer and James Choung share their honest, personal journeys, dig deeply into the character of God and his word,

and give an overview of global revival history to see what can be learned from it. And there is a lot! The book is brimming with thoughtful wisdom and experience, and is practical and visual in its explanations. As I read it I was challenged, convicted, and energized. This is revival theology at its best!"
Tor Erling Fagermoen, regional secretary IFES Europe

"It is so helpful when someone tackles a word or theme when there are so many opinions as to what it means. James and Ryan have done a great service to all of us by doing just that. As a friend once said to me, 'The problem with words is, you do not know where they have been.' This is a book that will feed the hungry pilgrim and renew a longing prayer that lies within so many hearts."
Phil Strout, national director, Vineyard USA

"For years now, I have been waiting for a book like this to come across my desk. As a pastor in a rapidly shifting context, I have myself been longing for revival, and this book has nourished my imagination. Revival can be an experienced reality today."

Tara Beth Leach, senior pastor of PazNaz, author of *Emboldened*

"There's no better time than the present for a grounded, holistic, and strategic book on revival. James Choung and Ryan Pfeiffer have masterfully crafted a timely book that deals with head, heart, and hands in sustaining times of revival. Longing for, pursuing, and persisting toward revival are important precursors to sustaining and multiplying a move of God's Spirit among a people. You cannot read their book on revival without being profoundly moved to pray, 'Lord, do it again!' Read this book, learn from their experiences, and be shaped through their insights into all it takes to be ready for a move of God."

Ed Stetzer, Billy Graham Distinguished Chair of Church, Mission, and Evangelism, executive director of the Billy Graham Center, Wheaton College

"This is a much-needed book to awaken our hearts with a longing for Jesus' glory to be revealed to a lost and broken world. Just a moment of his presence can transform a community, and this book will build your faith for another Great Awakening."
Gerard Long, president of Awakening to God Ministries, former president of Alpha USA

"Since college, Ryan and I have shared a heartfelt desire for transformation. Ryan has been a tireless fighter for change: in our lives, our families, our communities, and our world. Full of the fire for abundant life, Ryan remains a lifelong champion of revival, committed to the hope that something brighter is about to break through. The healer of souls is on the move! I hope that this book will ignite a fire in your soul to join the movement."
Jon Foreman, Switchfoot

ABOUT THE AUTHORS

James Choung (DMin, Fuller Theological Seminary) is vice president of strategy and innovation for InterVarsity Christian Fellowship/USA. He previously served as InterVarsity's national director of evangelism. He is the author of *True Story and Real Life*.

Ryan Pfeiffer is Next Gen pastor at North Coast Calvary Chapel in Carlsbad, California. He previously served with Inter-Varsity Christian Fellowship/USA as the divisional director for San Diego.

***

Please visit us at ivpress.com *for more information about James Choung and Ryan Pfeiffer and a list of other titles they've published with InterVarsity Press.*

Also Available from James Choung and InterVarsity Press

True Story: A Christianity
Worth Believing In

Real Life: A Christianity
Worth Living Out

Based on a True Story

Discover more titles from
InterVarsity Press

Click to view the newest and trending titles in

Academic Texts & Reference
IVP Academic covers disciplines such as theology, philosophy, history, science, psychology, and biblical studies with books ranging from introductory texts to advanced scholarship and authoritative reference works.

Culture, Mission, and Christian Life
Our books are deeply biblical and profoundly practical, discussing topics like Christian spirituality, prayer, evangelism, apologetics, justice, mission, and cultural engagement.

Bible Studies & Group Resources
IVP provides Bible studies and small group resources for you and your church, helping individuals and groups discover God's Word and grow in discipleship.

Spiritual Formation
Formatio books follow the rich tradition of the church in the journey of spiritual formation. These books are not merely about being informed, but about being transformed by Christ and conformed to his image.

Church Leadership
IVP Praxis brings together theory and practice for the advancement of your ministry using sound biblical and theological principles to address the daily challenges of contemporary ministry.

Click below to view more books in these categories

Apologetics	Discipleship	Philosophy
Biblical Studies	Family, Children & Youth	Psychology
Career & Vocation	Fiction	Race & Ethnicity
Church & Culture	Justice/Peace	Science
Church History	Spiritual Formation	Theology
Commentaries	Missions & Missiology	Youth Ministry

For a list of IVP email newsletters please visit ivpress.com/newsletters.

www.ingramcontent.com/pod-product-compliance
Lightning Source LLC
Chambersburg PA
CBHW011716220426
43662CB00018B/2392